GCSE
Media Studies

John Price

Text © John Price 2003

Original illustrations © Nelson Thornes Ltd 2003

The right of John Price to be identified as author of this work has been asserted by him
in accordance with the Copyright, Designs and Patents Act 1988.

Published in 2003 by:
Nelson Thornes Ltd
Delta Place
27 Bath Road
CHELTENHAM
GL53 7TH
United Kingdom

03 04 05 06 07 / 10 9 8 7 6 5 4 3 2 1

A catalogue record for this book is available from the British Library

ISBN 0 7487 6703 7

Illustrations by Steve Ballinger, Roger Wade Walker and Gary Slater

Page make-up by Paul Manning
Printed and bound in Croatia by Zrinski

Contents

Acknowledgements

The author and publishers would like to thank the following for permission to reproduce material: *The Daily Mail*, *The Guardian* and *The Observer*.

Every effort has been made to contact copyright holders and we apologise if any have been overlooked. Should copyright have been unwittingly infringed in this book, the owners should contact the publishers who will make corrections at reprint.

Picture credits

Action Plus Sports Images: p.22 (left and bottom right); p.24 (bottom)
Advertising Archive: p.1 (left); p.161 (left and middle left); p.163
Associated Press: p.18
BBC Picture Library: p.9 (top); p.10; p.15; p.23 (top left); p.31; p.32 (middle and bottom); p.33 (left); p.35; p.36; p.40 (left and top right); p.42; p.46; p.53 (right); p.177 (middle left); p.183
Ben Wright: p.183 (middle bottom)
Corbis: p.52 (left and bottom right); p.54
DC Thomson & Co Ltd: p.138
Digital Vision XA (NT): p.116
Emap magazines: p.118 (top right); p.119; p.126
Epic Scotland: p.17
Granada Media: p.33 (right); p.53 (left)
Jeremy Woodhouse/Digital Vision WT (NT): p.116
Kent News and Pictures: p.104
The Kobal Collection: p.60 (top right); p.69
The Kobal Collection/New Line/Dark Horse: p.60 (left); p.61
The Kobal Collection/Dreamworks LLC: p.60 (bottom); p.65; p.71 (left); p.75
The Kobal Collection/Columbia: p.63 (top)
The Kobal Collection/Ealing: p.63 (bottom)
The Kobal Collection/Universal: p.80
The Kobal Collection/Carolco: p.81
Magnum Photos/Peter Marlow: p.117 (top and bottom left)
Magnum Photos/Bruno Barbey: p.117 (bottom right)
National Magazine Company: p.125
Offside Sports Photography: p.1 (middle left); p.22 (top right); p.24 (top)
PC Gamer: p.188 (left); p.197
Rex Features Ltd: p.16; p.23 (middle and right); p.40 (bottom right); p.41; p.47; p.71 (right); p.72; p.73; p.99; p.146 (top right and bottom); p.148; p.150; p.158; p.177 (left); p.181
Science Photo Library: p.188 (right and bottom right)
Still Pictures/Tom Beer/Kate Watson: p.100
Still Pictures/Chris James: p.115
Still Pictures/Martin Harvey: p.116 (bottom right)
Stuart Higgins Communications: p.1 (right); p.161 (middle right); p.166
TOTP Magazine/BBC Worldwide Ltd: p.118 (left); p.130; p.146 (top left)
Topham Picturepoint: p.32 (top)
Vinmag Archive Ltd/20th Century Fox/Bongo Entertainment: p.1 (middle right); p.9 (bottom); p.132 (top right); p.134; p.135
Vinmag Archive Ltd/DC Comics: p.132 (bottom right); p.143
Vinmag Archive Ltd/Marvel: p.132 (left); p.142

Picture research by Sue Sharp

Introduction

You are likely to have a good knowledge of the media already, though not in an organised way. This book aims to help you use and develop that knowledge. It will show you how to describe and analyse media texts and how to make your own.

It aims to help you do well in your GCSE examination by developing your understanding of how and why media texts are produced, how people respond to them and what messages and values they contain.

You might be surprised to realise how much you already know about the media. Take the time to complete the activities at the end of this introduction – this should make you aware of the store of information and experience which you have accumulated through the years.

How to use this book

Each chapter of this book deals with a different **media form** or aspect of that form. That is, it separates television from radio, film from advertising, and so on. The aim of this is to make it easier for you to pick the parts of the book which are relevant to the course you are following.

In practice, the different media forms are often related. For example:

- Rupert Murdoch owns both BSkyB television and *The Sun* newspaper
- the *Spiderman* computer game is based on the film, which is in turn based on a comic
- advertising and news are featured on television and radio and in print.

This means that you sometimes have to combine material from different chapters.

Most chapters contain:

- ideas and advice about coursework
- background information
- examples of critical analysis of media texts
- ideas for production and pre-production work
- material for exam practice.

The term **media texts** is used to describe things like television and radio programmes, films, newspapers and magazines, recorded music, advertising, and so on. All of these 'texts' can be 'read' (interpreted) by audiences who understand the 'language' (sounds, visual images, words, etc.) which they use.

Key concepts

Below you will find a brief description of the main media concepts used in the text. These areas of study are indicated by icons in the margin as follows:

GENRE

This means 'type' and is about how people learn to classify media products, so that they can quickly tell the difference between, for example, a horror movie and a comedy, a television documentary and a soap opera, a teenage magazine and a DIY magazine, or a news broadcast and a quiz show.

It is also about how media producers repeat formats which they know are popular with audiences. Producers know, for instance, that TV quiz shows attract big audiences, so they keep producing them with variations on a basic format.

Genres have **conventions** that are understood by both the producers and the audience. For example, newspapers have headlines, photographs with captions, special sections for sport and so on.

Sometimes, especially in film, genres have certain images or details which are frequently used. These can be divided into three types:

- the physical attributes of characters and the way they dress and behave
- settings and locations
- the things which characters use.

This repetition of imagery is called **iconography**. For example, here is a description of the iconography of 1930s gangster films:

'In *Little Caesar* (1930) a police lieutenant and two of his men visit a night-club run by gangsters. All three wear large hats and heavy coats, are grim and sardonic and stand in triangular formation, the lieutenant at the front, his two men flanking him in the rear. The audience knows immediately what to expect of them by their physical attributes, their dress and deportment. It knows too, which is dominant, which subordinate.'

(Colin McArthur, *Underworld USA*)

NARRATIVE

This means how **stories** are organised. Stories can be found throughout the media: in news, drama, in documentaries, in sport and in advertising. The concept of narrative is about:

- how these stories are constructed, with beginnings, middles and endings
- topics such as **open** and **closed endings** (i.e. endings which leave you waiting for the next episode of a TV drama, as opposed to endings which solve the mystery or 'round off' the story)
- how stories are told (e.g. in films, time can be manipulated by flashbacks and slow motion)
- the kinds of characters there are in stories, and the roles they perform (e.g. heroes and villains).

REPRESENTATION

This means how the media portray people in terms of their gender, age, nationality and ethnicity. It is about values and beliefs, some of which are openly expressed and some of which are below the surface.

It can also be about the way the media portray issues and events – for example, the way newspapers depict asylum seekers or how television reports football hooliganism.

Two important related issues are **stereotyping** and **cultural diversity**:

- **Stereotyping** is a labelling process where people or groups are pigeon-holed and individual differences are ignored. It leads to generalisations ('teenagers are like this', 'foreigners/women are like that') which are usually critical or negative. It is often accompanied by prejudice.

- **Cultural diversity** refers to the portrayal of different communities and cultures in the media. There is a tendency for a dominant culture to be presented as normal and minority cultures (e.g. youth culture, black culture) to be presented as **deviant** (abnormal).

ORGANISATIONS

This is about how media products are made, advertised and sold. Key terms here are **marketing** and **promotion**. Study of media organisations could, for example, involve looking at all the ways films such as the *Harry Potter* films are **promoted** (advertised) and **marketed** (sold) through TV adverts, *Harry Potter* products in shops, computer games featuring the characters, videos and so on.

It is also about how the media are financed and controlled and includes topics such as **censorship**. The key terms here are **regulation**, **constraints**, **pressures**, **intrusion** and **privacy**.

- **Censorship** means not allowing people to hear, see or read something, usually because it contains bad language, violence or sex.
- The media are controlled by rules and laws. In the UK, for instance, there is a **libel law** which restricts what newspapers can write about people. There are also strict laws about the reporting of court cases.
- There are strict constraints imposed by the **Advertising Standards Association** on, for example, advertising aimed at children or adverts for alcohol.
- The **Press Complaints Commission** handles complaints about abuse of press freedom and sometimes tries to influence newspaper editors to stop them prying or intruding into famous people's lives.

AUDIENCES

This is about the consumers of the media, and how they use and interpret media products. Key terms include **uses** and **pleasures**. For example, study of media audiences could involve investigating whether computer games are stimulating or mind-numbing, or whether watching violent films makes people more aggressive (key terms: **reception** and **influence**).

It is also about how the producers of media texts target their products at particular sorts of people (the **target audience**), and about how those audiences are often 'sold' to advertisers.

Media producers no longer tend to think of a 'mass audience', but of 'the mass' being made up of distinct groups with different interests and needs.

The notion of audience is always closely linked with that of **organisations**.

Exam board categories

Use the table below to link the key concepts used in this book to the categories used by different examination boards:

Key concept	Examination Board Category		
	WJEC	**AQA**	**OCR**
Genre	'Media Texts'	'Media Language – forms and conventions'	'Languages and Categories'
Narrative	'Media Texts'	'Media Language – forms and conventions'	'Languages and Categories'
Representation	'Media Texts'	'Representation'	'Media Messages and Values'
Organisations	'Media Organisations'	'Institutions'	'Media Producers and Audiences'
Audiences	'Media Audiences'	'Audience'	'Media Producers and Audiences'

Activities

Collect and organise information about your media experiences.

Working in small groups, choose a different media form from the list below.

▶ *Construct a response to the questions on the media form your group has chosen.*
▶ *Present your findings as a poster to the rest of the class.*

Your poster should feature:

▶ *an image or picture*
▶ *brief text that can be read easily from a distance*
▶ *bright, co-ordinating colours which are eye-catching.*

Media forms

Television

▶ *List the types of programmes you watch (e.g. sport, quiz, news, etc.).*
▶ *List everything you know about one programme which you watch regularly.*
▶ *List the television personalities you like and dislike the most.*
▶ *What was your favourite television moment?*
▶ *List the different channels you have watched at some time or other.*
▶ *Describe the circumstances in which you watch TV (e.g. by yourself, with your family, while doing homework, etc.).*

Films

▶ *List the different types of films you have seen or know about (e.g. comedy, horror, sci-fi, action).*
▶ *Name your favourite film and write a paragraph explaining why you like it.*
▶ *List the film stars you **like** and **dislike** most.*
▶ *How do you watch your films (e.g. at multiplexes, on DVD, on television)?*
▶ *Write a paragraph explaining what you know about film-making and how it has developed and changed over the years.*

Radio

▶ *List the types of radio broadcasting you know about (e.g. music programmes, phone-ins, etc.).*
▶ *List all the radio stations you can receive in your area.*
▶ *Who is your favourite radio DJ/presenter, and why?*
▶ *What kinds of information can you learn from the radio (e.g. weather forecast, sports results)?*
▶ *Which radio programme do you like most, and why?*

Pop music

▸ *List the types of popular music you know (e.g. punk, reggae, blues, etc.).*

▸ *Which is your **favourite** and **least favourite** band/solo performer? Say why.*

▸ *List the different places where and ways in which you can listen to pop music.*

▸ *Write the words of any one pop song which you know by heart.*

▸ *Which recording means most to you, and why?*

Adverts

▸ *List the places where adverts can be seen.*

▸ *In your opinion, which is currently the most effective TV advert?*

▸ *Name an advert which persuaded you to buy what it was advertising.*

▸ *Which adverts have annoyed you?*

▸ *Describe your favourite advert.*

Newspapers and magazines

▸ *List all the newspapers and magazines you know.*

▸ *Which publications do you read regularly?*

▸ *List the types of things you can read in a national newspaper, a local newspaper and a teenage magazine (e.g. letters, advice, opinions).*

▸ *Which is your favourite magazine/newspaper, and why?*

Comics

▸ *List the types of comics you know (e.g. science fiction, children's, etc.).*

▸ *List the comic characters that you have heard of.*

▸ *Which is your favourite comic character, and why?*

▸ *List the comic conventions you know about (e.g. speech bubbles, frames, etc.).*

Computer games

▸ *List the **types** of games you know about (e.g. racing, strategy, etc.).*

▸ *Which is your favourite game, and why?*

▸ *In what circumstances do you usually play computer games (e.g. alone, with others)?*

▸ *Name some games based on TV or film characters.*

Internet

▸ *What do you mainly use the Internet for?*

▸ *Where do you use it?*

▸ *Which sites do you visit?*

▸ *What are your favourite websites?*

▸ *What controls do your parents impose on your use of the Internet?*

Production

Here is a production exercise which is fairly easy to organise but which will get you thinking about the main concepts involved in media studies.

Lifestory: prepare a display of photographs which will tell the story of your life.

This will involve:

▶ *selecting images from a range of choices*
▶ *deciding which form to use for displaying your images (e.g. storyboard, website, or magazine page)*
▶ *thinking about who you are preparing your story for – i.e. the audience*
▶ *ordering your images into a sequence which can be time-based, theme-based or random*
▶ *writing captions to explain or interpret the images*
▶ *deciding where to begin your story*
▶ *deciding whether to leave the story open-ended or finished.*

By deciding how to organise your images into a sequence, you are thinking about the media concept of **narrative** *(see above)*.

Your choice of images and captions involves thinking about how you want to be seen and understood by other people. This means thinking about the media concepts of **representation** and **audiences** *(see above)*.

Television: news

>> *This chapter covers:*

- television as a form
- how to analyse television news
- the regulation of TV news
- exam practice on news selection.

Television as a form

How does television differ from other forms of media? It is **mainly watched in the home**. This affects the nature of its programmes and schedules (the way they are timetabled). There is, for instance, a 'watershed' which means that programmes which are thought to be 'not suitable for children' are shown after nine o'clock.

Watching TV: a scene from *The Simpsons*

Viewers are **less attentive** than they are in a cinema. They are likely to be doing something else while they are watching. This means that programmes have to be devised to stimulate attention constantly in case people switch channels or decide to do something that seems more interesting.

This has an effect on **scheduling**. People need to know that a particular programme is on at a set time so that they can plan things like doing the washing-up. Programmes are made for particular times, such as children's television being scheduled at a time when most schoolchildren come home from school.

The **size of the screen** compared with a cinema screen makes a difference to the look of a programme. A small screen is better suited to showing conversations rather than broad landscapes and high speed action. This is why so much television shows people sitting around talking to each other. This has something to do with the way television employs a **direct look**. Newsreaders, reporters, and presenters talk directly to the camera in a way which is almost never used in cinema. Note, however, how television screens are being designed to look like cinema screens and some expensive sets are marketed as 'home cinema systems'.

Below: The cast of the TV soap *EastEnders*

British television history: some key moments

1936 BBC sets up first ever high-definition television service in the world. The service is only available in London and TV sets are so expensive that only a couple of hundred people can afford them.

1939 With the outbreak of World War II, BBC television is closed down amid fears that the transmitter at Alexandra Palace could act as a beacon for German aircraft.

1949 BBC begins transmissions to the Midlands. (It reaches Manchester in 1951 and Scotland, Wales and the West Country in 1952.)

1951 *What's My Line* becomes first of a string of popular TV game shows. Celebrities had to guess people's occupations. Ninety per cent of people with television sets watch the programme in 1952.

1953 Coronation of Queen Elizabeth II broadcast on TV. For the first time ever the broadcast of a state occasion has more TV viewers than radio listeners. In the weeks before the coronation an extra half a million TV sets are sold.

1954 First soap opera *The Grove Family* attracts nearly 9 million viewers.

1955 Start of ITV network.

Gibbs SR toothpaste is first product to be advertised on British TV.

1956 Introduction of videotape leads to cheaper editing processes and allows programmes to be prepared in advance.

1957 End of the closedown (between 6pm and 7pm so that parents could put their young children to bed).

First ITV super soap – *Emergency Ward 10*, set in a busy city hospital.

1960 Start of *Coronation Street.*

1961 First TV interview with a member of the royal family – the Duke of Edinburgh on *Panorama.*

1962 First satellite transmission. Viewers in Britain see brief live pictures from the USA via the Telstar satellite.

1964 BBC2 starts.

1965 *Till Death Us Do Part* – a new style of 'kitchen sink' situation comedy.

1966 *Cathy Come Home,* a drama about homelessness, has mass impact and causes outrage and anger. The homeless charity Shelter is consequently set up.

1967 Colour television arrives.

1969 Sony produces the world's first video tape recorder.

Monty Python introduces audiences to a new kind of surreal humour.

First live television pictures from the moon.

1974 Start of Ceefax and Teletext.

1975 First sensitive treatment of homosexuality in the drama *The Naked Civil Servant.*

1976 Britain's first black sitcom – *The Fosters*.

1980 Portrayal of Islamic justice in drama *Death of a Princess* causes diplomatic storm with Saudi Arabia.

First women leads in police shows such as *Juliet Bravo* and *The Gentle Touch.*

1981 Biggest television audience ever for wedding of Prince Charles and Diana.

1982 Start of Channel 4.

1983 Start of breakfast television.

1985 Live Aid concert raises £50 million for famine relief.

Start of *EastEnders.*

1988 Rescheduling of *Neighbours* at 5.25pm brings about a huge increase in audience.

1989 Start of satellite and cable television.

Television is **continuously available**. Unlike cinema-going, it is not regarded as a special event but is available on demand. This means the audience can be fickle, switching channels casually.

To counteract this, programme-makers tend to favour the series or serial so that people come to know when a certain programme or format is being broadcast and make an effort to organise their lives to allow them to watch it.

This has implications for the content of programmes so that the producers of soap operas, for instance, make viewers want to return day after day, week after week by planning 'cliffhanger' endings.

TV financing

The **financing** of television affects its programming. Some television is financed by taxation (the **licence fee**), while some is paid for by advertisers. Commercial television, which depends on money from advertising, is under pressure to produce popular programmes and is less inclined to provide for minority tastes. The BBC, on the other hand, because it receives its money from licence fees, does not have the same pressures to deliver big audiences to attract advertising. It is freer to broadcast less popular, minority interest programmes which commercial stations are reluctant to show.

Programme types

Certain **types of programmes** tend to dominate television schedules. There are many soap operas, quiz shows, situation comedies, talent shows and DIY programmes. This is due not only to their being popular, but also because they are cheap to make: it is much less expensive to produce a talk show with a presenter, a studio, and some members of the public than a costume drama filmed on several locations with a large cast of actors.

READING THE MEDIA
Analysing television news

Most people in the UK receive the bulk of their information about their region, their country, and other parts of the world from television news. It is important, therefore, to be able to analyse the programmes that provide us with so much information so that we can understand this information more clearly. This means knowing where the news comes from, how it has been selected, and how it is presented to the viewers. We need to learn whether television news is a 'window on the world' or whether, as Arthur Scargill said, 'What the BBC and ITN present as news is not news at all: it is pure, unadulterated bias.'

Watch four or five different news programmes from the same day's news. Select from different channels, different times, and different styles.

A useful combination would be:

▸ *GMTV's early morning news (ITV)*
▸ *any regional lunchtime news*
▸ Newsround *(BBC's news for young audiences)*
▸ Channel 4 News *(early evening)*
▸ The Ten O'Clock News *on BBC.*

Working in pairs or small groups, discuss in what ways these programmes are similar and different.

Try to agree on a list of **conventions** *that all news programmes must have.*

The checklist of TV news conventions below has been developed by media students. You may find it helpful to refer to during your discussion.

TV news conventions

- News programmes are about events that have happened recently.
- They are about important things like wars and crimes.
- There is either a single newsreader or a pair of newsreaders.
- The newsreaders talk directly to the camera unless they are interviewing someone.
- Reporters are introduced, who sometimes report live from locations where things of interest have happened.

- Sometimes members of the public are asked for their opinions.
- Sometimes experts give their opinions.
- There are usually moving pictures to illustrate the stories.
- There is usually music at the beginning and end of the programme, but not during it.
- Most stories are serious, but there is sometimes a light-hearted one at the end of the programme.

Describe introductions.

Listen carefully to the introductory music and describe what it is suggesting about the programme. Is it soothing or disturbing; tuneful or discordant; exciting or dull; instrumental or vocal?

Compare **introductory music** *from different news programmes and identify similarities and differences.*

The music is part of the branding process that makes each news programme distinctive. The word **branding** referred originally to the permanent marking of slaves or animals with a hot iron to show who they belonged to. It has come to mean a kind of trademark, a sign which is linked with a product so that people easily recognise it, e.g. the Macdonald's 'M' sign in red and yellow.

Are there any logos, colours, shapes, or words that tell you which channel you are watching?

Describe in detail the mise-en-scène and connotations of the sets.

The definitions below may help you.

MISE-EN-SCENE

This key media term comes from French cinema. It means everything that goes into the frames of a movie. This includes the sets or location, the set design, the costumes, and the props, as well as the acting style, the placement of cameras, the choice of lenses, and the lighting.

CONNOTATIONS

These are the meanings which different people bring to a word, image or sound. For example, the word 'green' is at a simple level a colour, but it could also mean or suggest 'go ahead', the countryside, Irishness, naivety and so on.

In news programmes, a background with the Houses of Parliament could suggest Britain, national power, or 'What follows will be dramatic and significant and you can trust us'.

A business-like environment with people working at computers in the background might suggest efficiency and professionalism – something like, 'What you are about to be told is important and there is an organisation working away now at the centre of power to keep you up to date'.

The **furniture** of the set and the background will be conveying messages too.

Look at the newsreaders.

▶ *How are they positioned? Do they sit, stand, or lounge about?*

Generally speaking, people who sit behind desks have a position of authority, e.g. most headteachers, many doctors, officials in benefits offices.

Behind the desk says, 'You'd better take notice of me because I'm an expert'.

Alongside a desk or perched casually on a desk suggests, 'I can be your friend' or 'We're all in this together'.

What sort of people are the newsreaders?

Describe them in terms of age, gender, ethnic/regional origin.

What sort of accent and what tone of voice do they have?

How are they dressed?

The BBC news used to be broadcast from a set with a long steel desk and with a blue background. This style was thought to be too cold and aloof, too machine-like. A softer, more relaxed atmosphere was needed.

The redesign introduced warmer colours: peach and maroon. The desk was made smaller and rounded to resemble two drums, which was in keeping with the drumbeats of the introductory music. Its circles recalled the circles representing transmission waves in the introductory visuals while the warm colours could be linked with the suggestion of a heartbeat in the introduction.

TV news presenters. *Left to right:* Moira Stewart, George Alagiah, Huw Edwards

The appearance of the presenter is all part of the message that is being broadcast. Viewers respond to these things in different ways. They may find the newsreader appealing and trustworthy, or they may be irritated and annoyed.

Producers of news programmes have to find newsreaders who appeal to large numbers of viewers and who have the ability to be serious and grave when reporting tragic stories but genial enough to read light-hearted stories. They also have to select teams of newsreaders so as to represent different social groups. There needs to be a balance of gender, age, ethnic groups and regional accents if particular sections of the community are not to feel excluded.

Consider how the stories are told.

The convention is for the newsreader to read out **headlines**. These are single-sentence summaries of stories and are intended not only to inform, but also to dramatise. They attract attention and encourage the viewer to stay with the programme.

Who else do the newsreaders introduce?

▶ *Newsreaders introduce **reporters**, who are usually where the story is happening, e.g. outside a courtroom, at the scene of a disaster, outside Number 10. The appearance or image of the reporters may be used to enhance a news item. For instance, if they are reporting from the scene of a military conflict the story can be made more dramatic if they wear bullet-proof clothing and a helmet, especially if there is some action in the background. On the other hand, such clothing would be no good for a reporter covering a royal visit to a new hospital!*

A viewer's reaction to a story can be affected by their response to the reporter. If you trust a reporter you are more likely to believe them than if you are suspicious of them.

Consider the response to the BBC's royal reporter Jennie Bond below.

▶ *In a group, discuss Anne Karpf's opinion of Jennie Bond. Which other royal reporters do you know? Who does the job most effectively? Why?*

Jennie Bond

JENNIE BOND IS ANOTHER GOOD REASON FOR A REPUBLIC

There are many things that would improve the quality of life but one simple act would do so at a stroke: removing Jennie Bond from our TV screens. ... Her style of reporting is nothing but lady-in-waiting journalism. ...

Her coverage of the Queen Mother's recent hospitalisation was typical. As usual Bond touted the Palace view – 'There's no sense of panic here; it's important to say that' – as though her role were to soothe public anxiety. She seemed like one of the Queen's retinue and admits to broadcasting as if the Queen were watching just over her shoulder.

Bond's language, her clothes and gestures all testify to a reporter who has gone native. As she stands before Buckingham Palace in a succession of bright, tailored suits, hands folded as if about to curtsey, she most resembles Princess Anne minus the curses.

How can we expect robust reporting of the monarchy from a journalist who also has to cover Ascot (and clearly loves it)? The qualifications

for that job are a thesaurus of synonyms for blue and a subscription to *Hats Monthly* ...

There's a real problem here about journalists and their sources and how far you can bite the hand that feeds you stories. This partly explains why Bond got the Charles and Diana story so spectacularly wrong for so long. But the royal family today needs the BBC more than the BBC needs the royal family, and the public needs a royalty correspondent rather than a royal one (with regal aspirations).

Bond's assumed stateliness isn't a new phenomenon. Newscasters from Alastair Burnett to Peter Sissons have read the news pompously, as if some of its gravitas might rub off on to them. On the other hand there's a new generation of women TV reporters like Margaret Gilmore and Philippa Thomas who are authoritative and inquiring but not grandiose. Next to them, Bond sounds pure Vera Lynn.

Anne Karpf
in The Observer 9 September 2001, page 22

Think about who else contributes to the news broadcast.

Experts are called on by the newsreader to explain situations and to analyse complex stories. On some news programmes they appear almost like lecturers or teachers standing at a blackboard. Mostly these experts are directly employed by the news organisation but sometimes they are freelances called in for particular stories, e.g. military experts explaining weaponry and battle tactics in times of war.

The reporter can give access to another voice by **interviewing** a person directly involved with the story. This person will not address the camera directly but will be shown talking to the reporter, thereby seeming to have less authority than the correspondent or newsreader.

Consider the importance of the visuals.

Television demands pictures, preferably moving ones, for its news programmes.

Look at one news programme and list the stories and the pictures that go with them.

Floods in Glasgow

▶ *Are the images:*

- *still or moving?*
- *live or recorded?*
- *recent or from a picture library or archive?*
- *taken by professionals or amateurs?*

How important were the pictures to the story? To what extent were they there just for something to see?

Some news programmes, such as CNN or BBC News 24, use the screen as a palette and show different bits of information at the same time in separate sections.

It is worth noting that the content of television news is very small compared with newspapers. Half an hour of television news is about the same as two-thirds of a broadsheet newspaper page.

Consider where the stories come from.

When you analyse a TV news programme you should try to work out how the reporters found out about each story.

Some are easy enough to detect: reporters seem to camp out at 10 Downing Street waiting for ministerial statements.

If you see reporters at the scene of an accident or fire, it is most likely that they will have learned about it from the emergency services, which have information lines. Reporters standing outside courtrooms will probably have just been attending a court case.

In some cases, however, the story's source is not revealed. Two out of every three news items come from **press releases** or **press conferences** and very few from journalists' own investigations. So the people who produce the press releases and organise the press conferences largely determine what we, the audience, see and hear.

Find examples of televised news conferences and try to decide who organised them and with what purpose.

The Conservative Chancellor of the Exchequer, Norman Lamont, issues a press statement outside the Treasury in Whitehall

Look at how a particular group, event, or issue is portrayed on TV news.

In particular, look at something which is controversial, for example:

- *immigration*
- *animal rights issues*
- *treatment of criminals*
- *pay disputes*
- *industrial action*

- *modern art*
- *protest marches*
- *the arms trade*
- *drugs.*

To what extent is the reporting balanced or biased?

Alternatively, you could follow the way in which a particular celebrity is portrayed.

This story concerns a girl called Nayirah and was first reported in *The Daily Telegraph* on 5 September 1990.

Iraqi soldiers reportedly entered hospitals in Kuwait and threw premature babies out of their incubators so that these incubators could be sent back to Iraq. The report was no more than a rumour, until a 15-year-old Kuwaiti girl appeared before the United States Congress to tell tearfully how she had seen these things happening.

Her terrible tale helped to persuade the American government to approve military action against Iraq.

Nearly two years later the truth emerged that the girl had been recruited and coached by a public relations firm, who had been paid $10 million to campaign for military intervention to oust Iraq from Kuwait.

The girl was, in fact, the daughter of the Kuwaiti ambassador to the United States.

Case Study
News management in wartime

How does the selection of news stories differ for different audiences?

Look for examples of younger audiences being given stories which are more relevant to their age group.

The 1990 Broadcasting Act states that broadcasters must observe 'due impartiality' in covering political issues.

In some countries (for example, communist and fascist states in the 1930s and 40s), broadcast news came under the control of authoritarian governments.

In Britain the political parties were keen to avoid the possibility of control of the broadcasting media falling into the hands of one or other political faction. Consequently the BBC came into being as an independent organisation, funded through the licence fee and protected from interference by the government of the day. The commercial **Independent Television Network**, which began in 1954, was also protected by law from being subject to political or economic pressure.

Until 2002, broadcasting was regulated by the **Independent Television Commission**, **the Broadcasting Standards Commission** and the **Broadcasting Complaints Commission**. The job of these bodies was to monitor broadcasts and ensure that they:

- were in good taste
- reflected a variety of interests and opinions
- were politically impartial.

These tasks are currently being handed over to a new organisation called **OFCOM**.

---

*Conduct your own **research** into what people think about local news programmes.*

▶ *David Morley in* Family Television *(Routledge 1986, page 169) found that women tended to prefer local news to national news, whereas with men the opposite applied.*

Interview *your own relatives to find if this is still the case where you live.*

MAKING THE MEDIA — News selection

You are the news editor of a breakfast TV magazine programme trying to appeal to a young audience as they get ready to go to school or work.

They do not want to watch ITV or BBC news and they are watching the magazine for fun as well as information. They are likely to be in a hurry so you have to keep your news bulletins short and snappy.

*From the list of available news stories below you have to **select a top five** and decide which order to put them in.*

You should give reasons for your selection and ordering.

▸ A 28-year-old man has been sacked for smoking cigarettes in his home. *(Two interviews, one with the man and one with his employer.)*

▸ A film star (your choice) has been given an engagement ring worth £75,000 by her partner (your choice). *(Pictures of the star and the engagement ring.)*

▸ The Queen is to visit the Coronation Street *set. (Library pictures of Queen and/or* Coronation Street *characters available.)*

▸ There has been a big increase in unemployment among the under-25s. *(Library pictures of interior of a job centre.)*

▸ The national minimum wage is to be increased by £1.

▸ A five-year-old girl has drowned during a school swimming lesson. *(Pictures of the school and swimming pool.)*

▸ Julia Roberts will earn £15 million for her next film. *(Publicity shots of Julia Roberts.)*

▸ Hollyoaks *star Joanna Taylor will be seen having a bath with a whole football team in a new storyline. (Publicity pictures available.)*

▸ A plane full of holidaymakers has crashed in the Indian Ocean killing all on board, some of whom were believed to be British. *(Dramatic amateur pictures available.)*

▸ A well-known married politician is having an affair with a stripper. *(Still pictures of the politician and the stripper.)*

▸ Twenty old-age pensioners have contracted a serious disease after a party in a residential home. *(Pictures of the exterior of the home – live report possible.)*

▸ A farmer in Devon has said he has definite proof that aliens have landed on his farm. *(Live interview can be arranged.)*

Write the script for a 30-second introduction to the news bulletin.

▸ *Give viewers the headlines and list the pictures which you would include.*

Design a web page for an Internet version of your selected news items.

▸ *See Chapter 15, pages 198–9, for advice on web page design.*

Exam practice ▬▬▬▬▬▬▬▬

Watch the opening of two contrasting national news programmes, for example *Newsround* and *Channel 4 News*.

1   Describe briefly the sets of the two programmes. Identify two similarities and
    two differences.

2   Describe the presenters and state how they might appeal to different target audiences.

3   You have been asked for your ideas for a local version of one of the programmes.

    a   Suggest a title.
    b   What introductory music/sounds would you use?
    c   What audience would you target?
    d   List three things you would include in your set which would emphasise
        its local nature.
    e   Who would you choose as presenter/s and why?

4   Which other media present the news? What advantages and disadvantages does TV news have in comparison with them?

Chapter 2

Television: sport

>> *This chapter covers:*

- how to analyse sport on TV
- pre-production work on planning a trailer for a new sports programme
- exam practice on analysing extracts from TV sport.

READING THE MEDIA — Sport on television

Television does not create sport, though it sometimes supports it financially. It reports sport. It shows sporting events live or with edited highlights, and we, the audience, seem to be seeing reality. But we have to understand that what we are shown is only a version of reality, and that this version depends on many factors such as camera positions, editing techniques, commentaries, expert analysis, interviews and so on.

Look carefully at two major TV sports programmes. One should be from commercial television and should include the advertising before, during and after the programme.

Describe and analyse the programmes using the headings and guidelines below.

TV sports presenters. *Left to right:*
Gary Lineker, Murray Walker,
Gaby Yorath

Presenters

The presenter has to address both the **specialist viewer**, who has a deep knowledge of the sport, and the **general viewer**, who is not an expert but wants to be entertained. The proportion of experts and general interest viewers will vary according to the programmes and the time they are shown.

The larger the proportion of general-interest viewers as opposed to specialists, the more likely it is that the presenter will promise excitement and drama, and emphasise personalities and celebrities.

Commentators and experts

Commentators have a privileged position: they are able to see both the live event and the television screen.

Find and list examples of commentators doing the following:

▸ *describing the venue, the atmosphere, and the action*

▸ *interpreting the event, e.g. 'That goal was ruled out because the forward was offside'*

▸ *providing **background information** – 'He's bowled him and that makes it the fifth time he's taken his wicket in this series'*

▸ *giving **professional insight** – 'Laura is taking a short iron so it looks as if she's going to lay up short rather than go for the green'.*

*Think about how far commentators **interpret** the event for you. In media studies this is called **anchorage**. In international fixtures, for example, how far are the commentators biased towards British teams and individuals in their interpretation of events?*

Experts are introduced to **predict** and **analyse** the event and to add comments during it. They are usually former sports stars themselves who have become media employees, for example Ian Botham in cricket, Gary Lineker in soccer, and Peter Alliss in golf. The fact that they were high achievers in their respective sports gives authority to their comments, although viewers may still reject their opinions.

Interviews

*Look for and describe examples of the **participants themselves being
interviewed** during pauses in the contests or, more frequently, when the event
has just finished.*

Spectators

*Describe how, if at all, **spectators** are used during live broadcasts.*

▶ *Does television use them simply for atmosphere or to seek their opinions?*

Openings and endings

*Compare the way the events are introduced and the way they are analysed at
the end of the programmes.*

▶ *Is there any difference between the people who are highlighted at the
beginning and those who are featured at the end? If so, why does this
happen?*

Personalities

*Some programmes focus on 'stars' at the expense of less famous team
members.*

▶ *Look for examples of how sports stars are 'built up' before an event, with
film of their past achievements to emphasise this.*

David Beckham

> *Sometimes these 'boosting' messages are
> reinforced after the event, but sometimes they
> are changed because of the sports star's
> failure to perform.*

▶ *Look for examples of how sports programmes concentrate on the
personal attributes (i.e. qualities and faults) of sportspeople.*

> *Sometimes, more attention is paid to
> sportspeople who have obvious or colourful
> character flaws because they make 'better copy'
> than people who are simply good at their sport.*

Tim Henman

Production techniques

*Find and describe examples of any of these techniques which were used in
the programmes you watched:*

- ▸ *long shots*
- ▸ *close-ups*
- ▸ *slow motion*
- ▸ *fast motion*
- ▸ *freeze frame*

- ▸ *steadicam*
- ▸ *miniature cameras*
- ▸ *tracking*
- ▸ *crane shots*
- ▸ *special editing effects.*

Choose two or three examples and describe the effect of the technique.

> *For instance, the use of a miniature camera fixed to a jockey in the Grand National might make the viewing experience more realistic, because it makes it seem as if you are actually taking part in the race. On the other hand, it can be irritating if you are trying to follow the progress of another horse.*

Target audience

You can form a clear impression of the target audience of a sports programme by studying the **advertising** that accompanies the programmes on commercial television. Sponsors' messages often portray the kinds of audiences a programme attracts. Carling advertisements, for instance, often feature young men on sofas watching sport on the television and drinking lager.

The **goods being advertised** will also give clues about the target audience. Playstation games suggests a largely young male audience; Ford Galaxy suggests adults with young families and well-paid jobs; whereas Nescafé coffee features young couples.

Make a list of all the adverts shown during a commercial sports broadcast and say what groups of people you think would be interested in each one.

> *One development that you could investigate is the way sports fans gather in public places in order to watch their sport as part of a group, e.g. 'Henman Hill' at Wimbledon.*

> *You could interview sports fans to see how they rate watching a sport on the television at home, in a crowded public place, or at the event itself.*

> *The use of wide-screen TVs in pubs for screening of sports events might also be worth investigating.*

Finance

Broadcasters sometimes pay a fee to gain exclusive rights to the event. There are three ways the broadcaster can recoup the money:

- the BBC uses money from the licence fee
- commercial television can operate a pay-per-view policy
- commercial television can 'sell' its audiences to advertisers.

How might the financial links between the broadcaster and the sport affect the presentation of the event?

> *For instance, if the broadcaster is earning revenue from advertising it would be in its interest to suggest that a boring event is just about to become more interesting so that viewers do not switch off.*

Look for and note any examples of presenters 'talking up' dull events during breaks.

Camera shots in sport

The programme's director will determine how the viewer sees the event. There will be either a wide variety of shots from which to select or on some channels the viewer will have a very limited choice of viewpoint.

This choice of viewpoint will affect how the event is interpreted. **Long shots** will be used in most sports to let the viewer see the overall progress of the event. But usually such shots will be interspersed with **close-ups** of contestants and sometimes officials and spectators. These are introduced either to clarify a controversial decision or to emphasise the dramatic and emotional aspects of the contest.

The **story** of the event will be partly determined by the selection of close-ups, which may focus on victory or defeat, triumph or despair, teamwork or individual skill, petulance or calm.

Encouraging viewer involvement

Sometimes the camera position can be chosen to allow viewers to feel as if they are taking part, as with the use of miniature cameras in cricket, motor-racing or horse-racing.

There is often use of **slow motion** and **freeze frame** to re-live key moments. The choice of which moments to replay and the commentary that goes with them will influence the way the sports event is interpreted. The use of close-ups and slow-motion replays allows viewers the luxury of being in a much better position to understand key moments than people actually attending the event .

Fast-motion editing involving a rapid mix of different camera angles and film/video clips is often used in programme introductions to grab the viewer's attention and stimulate interest and curiosity.

Trailer for a sports programme (pre-production)

Devise a 30-second trailer for the first television showing of a minority sport such as skateboarding. The programme will have celebrity contestants.

Produce a storyboard of your trailer, which should have between 15 and 25 different images.

*Decide on your **target audience** and when the programme will be scheduled.*

▶ *__Interview__ members of the target audience and find out what they want to see.*

▶ *Do they want explanations of the sport, for instance? Summarise your findings.*

*Decide which **celebrities** you wish to take part and give reasons for your choice.*

*Decide how you will make the sport sound interesting for a **non-specialist audience**.*

▶ *When the Football World Cup was advertised in 2002, the images were of great goals from past competitions, moments of individual skill, and celebrations by winning teams. Look at current sports programme trailers. What do they emphasise?*

▶ *What **sound effects** and **music** will you use? What atmosphere will they convey?*

*Write the anchoring **soundtrack**. What words will be spoken and by whom?*

*Write an **evaluation**.*

▶ *For advice on writing evaluations, see page 51.*

A sample storyboard is reproduced on pages 28–29.

'Come on, let's get on stage.'

Example of a storyboard

A storyboard is the first step towards visualising a script: a necessary stage of getting the ideas for a film or video on to paper.

The storyboard consists of a visual plan of each shot in terms of camera angles and what each frame contains. This plan can be referred to by the director and camera-person during the filming process.

In the pre-production stage a storyboard is especially important, but you do not have to be a great artist to produce a good storyboard. The sequence illustrated here – of two band members wandering in the backstage area of a concert venue – could be illustrated just as well with simple matchstick figures.

'I'm sure it's this way.'

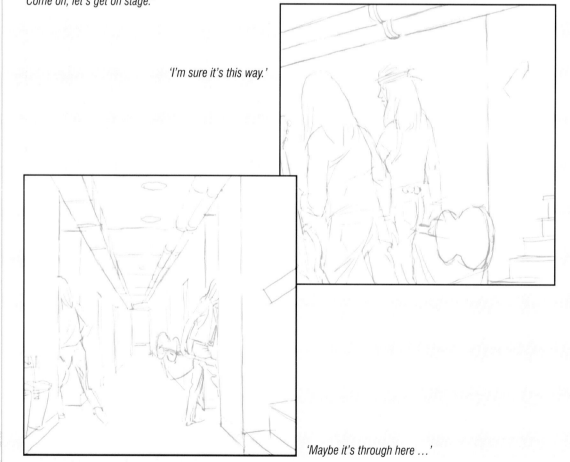

'Maybe it's through here ...'

'Do you think they might start without us?'

'We're going round in circles.'

'Maybe we'll get there for the encore.'

Exam practice ■■■■■■■■■■■■■

Record two 3-minute extracts from contrasting sports programmes,
e.g. soccer and snooker; tennis and golf; athletics and wrestling.

1   List three camera shots used in the extracts and explain why they have
    been used.

2   **a**   Suggest a title for a television sports programme for your locality.
    b   On which channel would your programme appear and at what
            time?
            Explain your choice.
    c   Which sports would you feature in your title sequence and why?
    d   Design a storyboard for your title sequence, identifying key shots
            and the soundtrack.
    e   Give three reasons why your programme would appeal to a
            particular target audience.

3   How are individual sportspeople represented? Are they represented as
    heroes, villains, clowns, victims, cheats, special, ordinary, etc?

4   How is the sport itself represented? Is it portrayed as drama,
    excitement, full of suspense, silly, pointless or fun?

5   Choose any televised sport and explain how it appeals to a television
    audience.

Television: situation comedy

>> *This chapter covers:*

- analysing situation comedies
- how situation comedies have changed over time – *The Royle Family* and *Rising Damp* as a case study
- situation comedy openings
- how to write a treatment for a situation comedy.

READING THE MEDIA

TV situation comedies

Typical features of situation comedies

Situation comedies on television grew from radio comedy programmes in the 1950s, when *Hancock's Half Hour* was transferred from radio. They are now classed by television companies as light entertainment rather than drama. They are often seen simply as programmes to make people laugh and escape from the worries of everyday life. But are they just escapist or do they have an influence on the way viewers see themselves, the groups they belong to and the world around them? The activities below are designed to help to answer these questions.

Make your own definition of situation comedy

Working in pairs or small groups, make a list of programmes which you would call situation comedies.

Discuss their similarities and differences.

▸ *Try to agree on a definition, but take note of any programmes that do not fit easily into the definition. The checklist below has been developed by media students – you may find it helpful to stimulate your discussion.*

TV sitcom
conventions

Situation comedies are programmes which:

- are meant to make you laugh
- focus on family life
- are sometimes set in the workplace
- have few sets, which are used over and over again
- tend to be shown during peak viewing times
- are realistic
- appeal to a family audience
- are acted out
- tend to last for half an hour
- are on mainstream television
- are on at the same time every week
- are easy to understand
- are entertaining
- have canned laughter

Compare sitcoms from different periods, noting similarities and differences.

View two sitcoms, one recent and one from the past.

▸ *Describe the sets and locations (**mise-en-scène** – see page 14). What similarities and differences do you find?*

*Describe the **camera techniques** which are used.*

> *Make a note of where the cameras are placed during filming and what sorts of shots they take. Compare and contrast the two programmes you are studying.*

*What do you learn about the **social class** and **attitudes** of the characters from the costumes and make-up?*

> *For example, Jim Royle's sloppy appearance might indicate laziness, whereas Rigsby's shabbiness probably emphasises his meanness.*

Popular TV sitcoms. *Top to bottom: Friends, The Royle Family, Only Fools and Horses*

Sitcom characters:
Royle: lazy. Rigsby: mean

Sitcoms which have not yet established themselves with TV audiences tend to use the same sets over and over again and rarely use outdoor locations. This is because their budgets are limited and using the same sets helps to keep production costs down.

> *In* The Royle Family, *for instance, we never leave the house and for most of the time we see only the living and dining area and part of the kitchen. In* Rising Damp *the acting space is equally confined to the dark and cramped rooms of a lodging house.*

However, a successful long-running situation comedy, such as *Only Fools and Horses*, will be able to afford some filming on location. There may also be special editions of such comedies at Christmas and Easter, which will tend to make more use of location filming.

It used to be conventional for comedy to be filmed mainly in medium shot with very few close-ups. Some recent comedies have used different techniques, with hand-held cameras and more close-ups.

Case Study
Rising Damp (1970s) and The Royle Family (from 2001): changes in camerawork

Rising Damp is filmed in a series of three-sided sets which represent the interior of Rigsby's boarding house. We know they have three sides because we are never shown the side from which the cameras film. It looks as if there are three cameras placed at different angles with the separate shots edited together later. Often a scene starts with someone coming in from a door at the side of the set.

The whole style of filming suggests the theatre. We, as viewers, are like a theatre audience watching from the auditorium as scenes are acted out before us. The programmes were recorded in front of a studio audience, and the audience laughter makes it seem as if we are watching with other people.

The Royle Family is filmed in a very different style. The camera is always at the level of the characters, which makes it seem as if we are sitting down with them. This makes us feel like part of the family rather than mere spectators.

Rising Damp and The Royle Family: contrasting sets

In *Rising Damp* the house is dark, old-fashioned, and cramped, indicating Rigsby's meanness. The basic furnishings and equipment are often faulty, with door handles coming off, beds collapsing, and water pipes leaking. These defects can be used for visual humour.

In *The Royle Family*, the home is poor but comfortable and the television set is the focal point. There is a casual shabbiness about the home, shown by the overflowing ashtray, the partly scraped walls (the family are planning to improve things by papering with woodchip), and the cluttered kitchen.

There seems to be a difference between long-lasting situation comedies such as *Friends*, *Frasier* and *The Royle Family*, and those which are short-lived.

*In some situation comedies there is a **main character** whose experiences and attitudes are central to the humour. Such characters perform like comedians on a stage. In other sitcoms, there are two main **characters who work as a pair**. The comedy depends on discussions, banter, and conflict between the two.*

*Sometimes there is more of an **interacting group**, which can be a family, friends or people who work together. Different **locations** produce different sorts of problems and give rise to different sorts of interaction.*

*Some situation comedies combine family and **workplace**, and thereby increase the range of topics and humour.*

- In the past, *Absolutely Fabulous* switched between Edina's home kitchen and the offices of her PR business.
- *Frasier* depicts both the main character's home and the radio station where he works.
- *The Simpsons* shows us Homer's home life and his work at the nuclear plant in Springfield.

Some situation comedies are based on a group of people who are not related but share the same accommodation. The humour often revolves around the problems of communal living. Examples of such programmes are:

- *The Young Ones*, a sitcom about a bizarre group of students
- *Porridge*, portraying a group of prisoners
- *Auf Wiedersehen Pet*, concerning a group of migrant building workers
- *Friends*, about six young people sharing accommodation in New York.

Study an episode of your favourite sitcom and complete the activities below.

Make notes about:

▶ *the problems or complications which arise. How are these sorted out by the end of the programme?*

▶ *the story. Is the narrative complete (**closed**) or left unresolved (**open-ended**)?*

*Describe the **main characters** and the way they behave.*

*Is there a **main character**, a **duo** or a **group**?*

*Are there any of these (or other) **character types**?*

▶ *the loveable scoundrel*
▶ *the doddery, slow-thinking, rambling old man*
▶ *the stressed mother*
▶ *the pompous but ineffective authority figure*
▶ *the petulant teenager.*

*Is the comedy set in a **family group**, in the **workplace** or in a **communal living setting**?*

*What do the sets indicate about the **people who live in them**?*

*Find examples of **jokes** based on:*

▶ ***misunderstandings** linked with character traits, e.g. in* Fawlty Towers, *Basil Fawlty is a snob who crawls to well-bred people, but in one episode is taken in by a conman who poses as a lord*

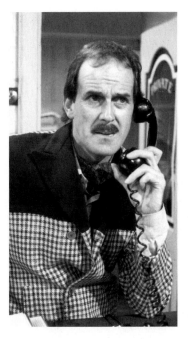

John Cleese as Basil Fawlty in
Fawlty Towers

▶ ***reversal of expected roles**, e.g. Edina the irresponsible middle-aged woman with the sensible teenage daughter in* Absolutely Fabulous

▶ *the **absurd**, e.g. Vyvyan eating the television set in* The Young Ones *when the television detector van comes round*

▶ ***things going wrong in the physical world**, e.g. the various mishaps that befall Frank Spencer in* Some Mothers Do 'Ave 'Em

▶ ***language-based** jokes, such as puns, double meanings, banter, and insults.*

Depending on your choice of sitcom, describe how either: i) a family, ii) an ethnic group, or iii) a gender is portrayed.

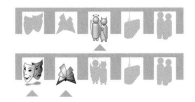

Traditionally in sitcoms the stories are **episodic**: each programme is self-contained and the **characters do not change** or develop but remain the same. That seems to be true of *Rising Damp*, where certain situations are constant, e.g. Rigsby always trying to woo Miss Jones.

In *The Royle Family*, however, there is some **continuity** and **development**. We seem to move through the family's lives with key times such as the wedding of Dave and Denise and the birth of their baby. However, the basic attitudes of the characters stay the same.

Look at how families are represented.

▶ *Do they appear 'normal' or unconventional?*

▶ *What sorts of family problems are dealt with?*

▶ *Is the family represented as essentially loving and supportive or always bickering and fighting?*

Consider how ethnicity is portrayed.

▶ *Which ethnic groups are shown?*

▶ *What characteristics of the ethnic group are emphasised?*

▶ *Is there any stereotyping?*

Think about how social classes are represented.

▶ *Do you notice any stereotyping of social classes?*

▶ *What social classes and which regions are shown?*

▶ *In work-based sitcoms, how are conflicts between workers and management portrayed?*

> **Work-based situation comedies often used to depict bosses as eccentric and incompetent.**

How far do current sitcoms concentrate on people's relationships rather than deal with important social issues such as equal pay for women?

Consider how gender is portrayed.

How are males and females represented?

▶ *In older situation comedies, women were often portrayed either as naive and stupid or as bossy harridans. More recently, men seem to be depicted as silly and irresponsible, while women are sensible, stable and practical.*

Investigate sitcom audiences.

Find out if there is a difference between male and female attitudes to situation comedies.

▶ *Some research by David Morley, reported in* Family Television *(page 170), showed that adult female viewers especially disliked unrealistic comedies such as* The Young Ones:

> 'A significant number of women interviewed display a strong dislike of "zany" comedy as a genre, and of *The Young Ones* in particular as an instance of this genre. On the other hand, their husbands, sons and teenage daughters all tend to like this type of comedy very much.'

Morley believes that because women are mainly responsible for order in the home, they find the idea of domestic chaos shown in The Young Ones *insulting.*

Interview five males and five females and make notes on their attitudes to sitcoms.

▶ *Find out their likes and dislikes, and draw conclusions about any gender differences that you find.*

Why are successful long-running situation comedies relatively cheap to produce?

Write a paragraph about the re-use of sets, the small casts, the size and predictability of the audience, and the lack of location filming.

MAKING THE MEDIA

Write a treatment for a TV situation comedy.

*A **treatment** is a plan or set of intentions.*

TARGET AUDIENCE

First, choose the kind of audience you are aiming at.

▶ *It could be a mainstream, family audience, or a specialised, limited one such as teenagers or young children, or one based on ethnic origin or geography.*

SETTING

After deciding upon your target audience, decide what setting you will use: family, workplace or communal group. Then try to be more specific:

▶ *If you decide on a communal group, what brings the group together, and where?*

▶ *If you choose family, what type of family? Conventional or unconventional; with children or childless; which social class; what sort of financial circumstances?*

▶ *If you choose a workplace, what sort of work is going on?*

CHARACTERS

What characters will you have?

▶ *Will the comedy be based around a single main character, a pair or a group?*

Write profiles of your main characters.

▶ *To what extent will they conform to basic types or be unique individuals?*

▶ *How will your characters dress to indicate their characteristics? Illustrate with drawings.*

▶ *What faults will your characters have that will lead to complications in the stories?*

▶ *Which actors will you use?*

SET DESIGN

What will the sets look like?

Produce illustrations to show sets and costume.

TOPICS

What will the topics for your stories be?

FILMING

How will you film your programmes in terms of studios, locations and types of camera shots? Give reasons for your decisions.

Write a report to evaluate your pre-production.

You should include:

▸   *the generic conventions you have used*
▸   *the storylines*
▸   *how effectively you managed to attract and to please your target audience*
▸   *what could be improved*
▸   *how far your programme relates to current media output.*

For advice about evaluations, see page 51 (Chapter 4).

Television: quiz shows

>> *This chapter covers:*

- how to analyse TV quiz programmes
- background information about *Who Wants To Be A Millionaire?*
- a structure for comparing two current quiz programmes
- ideas and advice for producing your own TV quiz programme
- exam practice.

READING THE MEDIA

TV quiz shows

Quiz shows are just one genre of television programme which involve competition. They have the same kind of appeal as sports programmes and reality television, with the audience placed in the position of being judges, able to sit back and assess performance and sometimes influence outcomes. Although there are similarities between these programmes, there are also clear distinctions. The activities below will help you to recognise these.

Identify quiz show conventions.

Working in small groups or in pairs, make brief notes about the content and style of quiz shows you are familiar with.

Discuss how many of the characteristics listed below would you expect in a TV quiz show. Are there any others that are missing?

- questions and answers
- prizes
- a presenter
- jokes
- music
- sound effects
- interviews
- an audience
- contestants
- problems to solve
- physical challenges
- competing teams
- songs
- conjuring tricks
- news stories
- clowns
- glamorous women

Now try to **write a definition of a quiz show** *based on your answers.*

▶ *How many of the characteristics were you not sure about?*

▶ *How easily do the programmes you thought of fit into your definition?*

Describe and analyse the conventions of a contemporary quiz show using the questions below.

What kind of person presents the show, and how is he or she dressed?

Consider the age, gender and ethnicity (racial origin) of the presenter.

What role does the presenter play?

▶ *Possible roles are:*

- *helper*
- *entertainer*
- *referee*
- *judge*
- *taskmaster/mistress.*

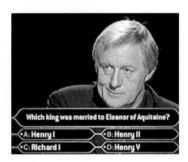

Chris Tarrant, presenter of *Who Wants To Be A Millionaire*

▶ *The presenter can be in charge of the knowledge and act like a schoolteacher who knows the answers and dishes out praise or punishment. Anne Robinson in* The Weakest Link *plays the role of a severe and sarcastic headmistress dishing out mainly punishment.*

▶ Millionaire's *Chris Tarrant in contrast is more genial. He does not see the correct answers until we do. Although he sometimes teases contestants, he is more usually in the role of* **helper**.

▶ *The way the presenter is **dressed** may be significant.*

> *Chris Tarrant wears suits which blend in with the main colours of the set: blue and purple. Sometimes he wears a gold or silver tie, which might suggest money or wealth.*

> *Anne Robinson dresses in black, loose-fitting clothes that are similar to an academic gown. She wants to appear stern and remote.*

▶ *Presenters are often comedians, such as Bob Monkhouse, who entertain the viewers with jokes and banter.*

*How important is the **set design** and general **mise-en-scène**?*

▶ *Look in particular at the positioning of the contestants and the presenter. Often, greater tension is created by making the contestant appear vulnerable or alone. The positioning of the audience can be important too. In some quiz shows, the audience takes part.*

▶ *Describe any special lighting effects.*

How are tension and suspense created?

▶ *In most quiz shows, the contestant appears under pressure. This can be a time pressure or a physical pressure. The idea is to increase the tension for the viewer.*

▶ *Situations can be made more tense by making the contestant appear isolated. In* Mastermind, *this is achieved by using a black leather chair in a darkened room with a bright light shining on the contestant and the camera zooming in very slowly as the questions progress.*

▶ *What part does the increasing value of the prizes play?*

▶ *Does the editing of the programme use the delaying effect of commercial breaks to heighten suspense?*

In your chosen contemporary quiz show, what different camera shots and techniques are used?

▶ *Look for examples of close-ups, slow zooms as tension increases, and fast-moving crane shots to create excitement.*

*How are **background music** and **sound effects** used?*

> *Some quiz shows add music during the questions to make them seem more dramatic. Sometimes sounds are used to indicate different stages of the game.*

Anne Robinson, presenter of
The Weakest Link

A tense atmosphere is achieved in *Millionaire* by having a circle in which the contestant sits, perched on a high stool and surrounded by a dimly lit audience. There are lots of connotations here and viewers will differ in their interpretations. The set could be a stage, a ring in which fighting takes place, or, when the blue lights shine on it, a pool that you can sink into. It suggests a place of both opportunity and danger. The idea of danger is reinforced by the offer to the contestants of 'lifelines' ('Phone a Friend', 'Ask the Audience' and 'Fifty-fifty'). So the audience are really watching a 'struggle to survive'.

On the other hand, the golden pillars and staircases which lead up to a starry background suggest a stairway to a new life and represent opportunities and dreams. This set is different from the set of *The Weakest Link*: while the *Millionaire* set gives the impression that contestant and audience are in this tense situation together, the *Weakest Link* set emphasises separation and competition.

Millionaire uses a combination of lighting, sound and camera movements to make the quiz more dramatic.

The original pilot shows were thought to be too brightly lit and did not have enough music. Brian Pearce, the lighting director, was brought in to 'throw away conventional lighting and come up with something completely different'. He used beams of light moving like searchlights and darkened the studio audience area. Other programmes have copied the lighting styles of *Millionaire*.

---

*How far is each programme giving a series of '**mini-stories**'?*

▸ *Look at the way contestants are introduced. Note the sorts of things that are mentioned and those that are ignored.*

▸ *In* Millionaire *we are introduced to a person who becomes the **hero** or **protagonist**. Chris Tarrant talks to people about their personal ambitions and dreams. In this way, the viewer at home can identify with the contestants.*

▸ *Why does Chris Tarrant introduce a relative or friend who sits in the audience and is featured from time to time during the programme?*

Often Chris Tarrant stresses the financial links between the contestant and their friend or relative with statements such as:

> *'They're planning to get married in May, and if they win the money, they're not planning to bring the wedding forward, but Anita (who is in the audience) is planning to bring the hen night forward.'*

The contestant's story is added to by having a friend or relative in the audience. This person is pictured at crucial stages of the contest.

*What are the **underlying values** of the programme?*

▸ *How far does the programme show approval of **competition**?*

▸ *Are people competing against other contestants or against impersonal forces such as 'the computer'?*

▸ *Do quiz programmes reflect a belief that everyone has a chance but only a few get to the top because they know more or work harder?*

*What sort of **knowledge** is valued?*

▸ *Is it fair to say that successful quiz show contestants simply store knowledge in the way that squirrels store nuts?*

▸ *How far does the quiz show test speed of recall rather than **ability to reason** and think?*

In Family Fortunes, *the valued knowledge is of public opinion. Contestants have to guess the results of public opinion polls; popular **common sense** rather than specialist knowledge is encouraged.*

The Weakest Link *and* Who Wants to Be A Millionaire *test stores of what some might describe as **trivial information**.*

In The Price is Right, *knowledge of the prices of goods in the shops is valued. This programme is usually shown during daytime television, when the viewers will be mainly the members of the household who are the main shoppers. Here, a **social skill** is being valued rather than factual knowledge.*

*How important are the **prizes**?*

▸ *Do quiz programmes encourage **greed** and glorify consumer goods and money?*

▸ *To what extent are audiences attracted by the size of the prize money?*

▸ *Carry out your own survey of this aspect of quiz shows by asking regular quiz viewers what they think and summarise your findings.*

Quiz show finance

Quiz shows are particularly suited to television because they are **popular** and they are relatively **inexpensive** to produce. Sometimes, they draw huge audiences, which commercial television can 'sell' to advertisers.

Advertising revenue

The cost of **advertising** in commercial breaks is based on the size and content of the audience (the people watching at home). Advertisers buy time for their adverts to be shown and pay according to the size and composition of the audience. Advertising can also be in the form of sponsorship of programmes, which works in a similar way.

The BBC does not get its money from advertising, but it still tries to attract big audiences. It has to be popular to justify the **licence fee** which owners of television sets have to pay. So when it finds a successful format like *The Weakest Link* it uses it to encourage people to switch to BBC, particularly at crucial times such as the early evening. It is important to attract large audiences at this time because they are then likely to stay tuned to the same channel throughout the rest of the evening.

Production costs

Quiz shows are inexpensive to produce because they are **studio-based**. They can use the same set over and over again. The staffing costs are low compared with, say, a drama. Quiz shows are much less complicated in terms of organisation and equipment than a sports outside broadcast, for instance. Several programmes can be filmed in a single day and broadcast at a later date. The prize money, though often small, can be financed from advertising or phone calls from viewers.

Selling the format

A successful format for a quiz show can be sold to other countries. Over 50 countries have bought the *Millionaire* format from its originators, the production company Celador. Some changes are allowed for cultural reasons, but the logo, set, music and lighting have to be the same as the original. There can also be large financial returns on **merchandising**, for example the *Millionaire* board game was the most popular Christmas gift in 2001.

Quiz show audiences

Quiz show viewers **become involved** emotionally, feeling excitement if people win and sadness if they lose. The viewers can be encouraged to identify with the contestants, so that they may want a particular person to win because they come from their own area, or because they are out of work, or because they look attractive.

In *Millionaire*, the viewers are encouraged to become involved by being positioned as if they are **participating**. The possible answers to the questions are shown on screen. According to the producer David Briggs, 'People can't stop themselves shouting the answers at the television.'

The show is also about 'pushing people's emotions close to the limit. It's all about seeing people make **life-changing decisions** before your eyes. That's why the size of the prize money is so important,' says Briggs.

In *The Weakest Link*, on the other hand, viewers can take a sadistic pleasure in the embarrassment and **failure** of the contestants, with Anne Robinson scolding them for being incompetent. She dismisses them harshly and abruptly when they fail:

'You *are* the weakest link. Goodbye.'

Contestants

If quiz show contestants are **ordinary**, the television audience can find it easier to feel as if they are part of the show because they can imagine competing themselves. On the other hand, the audience can also admire **experts**. *Mastermind* was popular although most viewers would have had no idea about the answers to some of the very obscure special subjects that contestants chose.

Some programmes, such as *Fifteen to One*, use contestants who are quiz experts, whereas others use non-experts. This choice affects the audience response. Some viewers admire people who know a lot, while others prefer to identify with contestants who are 'brave triers' and need help from the audience or a friend. Others might like to see people humiliated.

Sometimes, there is an economic purpose to choosing non-expert contestants, as 'ordinary' people feel encouraged to ring in to the programmes to see if they can take part. The programme-makers can earn lots of money from these calls, as the greater the number of people that feel that anyone can take part and with luck be successful, the more phone calls there will be and the more revenue for the production company.

Audience participation

The behaviour and reaction of the **studio audience** is an important ingredient in the appeal of different quiz show formats.

- The *Mastermind* audience comprised university staff who were polite and restrained.
- In *Millionaire*, the audience are potential participants who can be asked to help as one of the contestant's three 'lifelines'.
- In less formal shows like *Play Your Cards Right* the audience is sometimes encouraged to be noisy and to shout responses.

The key point is that the participation or otherwise of the audience will have been planned by the programme's producers and will have different effects on the viewers at home. The programme-makers might intend to create tension or excitement, and the viewers at home will react to this in different ways, some becoming engrossed and some indifferent. Alternatively, they might simply want audiences to be amused or entertained. Celebrity quiz shows and satirical quiz shows such as *Have I Got News For You* are two such examples.

Paul Merton, one of the regular panellists on the satirical TV quiz *Have I Got News For You*

WHO WANTS TO BE A MILLIONAIRE

Because of the big cash prizes offered, the show has to be financed by revenue from telephone calls.

Callers to *Who Wants to Be A Millionaire* are greeted by the recorded voice of Chris Tarrant. After pressing telephone keys to indicate which show they want to be on, they are asked a test question. If they answer it correctly, they hear a congratulatory message and are told that the production company, Celador, may select them as a contestant. Finally the voice wishes them good luck.

By November 2000, during the eighth series of the show, phone calls from would-be contestants had contributed more than £20 million in revenue. After VAT and phone company charges, £7.69 million went to pay for publicity, the cost of selecting the contestants and prize money.
At that time, the average cost of a phone call to the show was 76p.

The show is recorded the day before it is shown. Friends who are phoned genuinely have only 30 seconds to help.

A garden designer from Fulham was the first contestant to win £1 million. In November 2000, Judith Keppel answered all fifteen questions to win the top prize. Her £1 million question was: 'Which king was married to Eleanor of Aquitaine?' She had to choose from Henry I, Henry II, Richard I, and Henry V.

In September 2001, a £1 million prize was withheld from a 'winner', Charles Ingram, because he was getting help from his wife and another contestant, Tecwen Whittock. They used a series of coughs to guide Ingram to the correct answers. In April 2003 all three were found guilty of trying to procure a million pounds by deception.

While the show is in production, over 5,000 lines are available to aspiring contestants nationwide. Of these,100 are selected at random and 10 each day are invited to participate.

'It is perfect television of its kind. It's so simple, yet so gripping,' according to Garry Bushell, TV correspondent of *The Sun*.

Compare two current TV quiz programmes.

The questions below may help you.

GENRE

What are the defining features of quiz programmes?

▶ *Think about rules, prizes, presenters, music and sound effects, and so on.*

▶ *Describe the presenters and the way they are dressed, noting any differences.*

▶ *Describe the contestants.*

▶ *Describe the sets and suggest why they have been designed in this way.*

▶ *Describe technical effects such as lighting, sound and camera movements, and explain why they have been used.*

NARRATIVE

▶ *Describe examples of mini-stories with contestants as 'characters'.*

▶ *Describe any roles which the presenters perform, such as helper, authority figure, comedian or trickster.*

▶ *How are the programmes edited and organised to create conflict and suspense?*

AUDIENCES

▶ *What audience are the programmes principally aimed at in terms of age, gender and ethnic origin?*

▶ *How can viewers get involved in the programmes?*

▶ *Do the programmes involve a studio audience? If so, how do the audience participate?*

REPRESENTATION

Explain the underlying values of the programmes.

▶ *Consider issues such as greed, competition, co-operation, cruelty, compassion and fun.*

 What sort of knowledge is valued?

 How important are the prizes?

ORGANISATIONS

▸ *Which channel are the programmes on, and how does this affect the financing of each programme?*

▸ *When are the programmes scheduled, and why?*

▸ *Describe any merchandising connected with the shows.*

▸ *How are production costs for the programmes kept low?*

Find out why people like a particular quiz programme.

▸ *Choose people who are keen fans of the programme. Find out what they think about the presenter, the contestants, the kinds of prizes awarded and the production values (such as sound, lighting, camerawork).*

▸ *Interview them in depth and record the interviews so that you can analyse them carefully when you have time. Your role is to encourage people to talk openly, so do not challenge or argue. Try to ask questions which prompt people to say more.*

▸ *How far do they become involved in the programme?*

▸ *Ask them about the conditions in which they view the programme. For example, what time of day, whether they watch while they are doing something else, who else is watching, and so on.*

Write a report on your findings.

(See Chapter 7 for advice about camerawork.)

MAKING THE MEDIA | **A quiz programme (production)**

Produce a basic quiz programme.

Here is a basic exercise in production, for which you need a camcorder, a space and some friends. It would be useful if you also had an extra camera, a tripod, some lighting equipment and an extra microphone, but these are not essential.

Your aim is to produce part of a quiz programme lasting a few minutes and involving two contestants. The scoring will be like a game of noughts and crosses. You need an empty grid with one person being **X** and the other being **O**. Each correctly answered question fills a space in the grid and the first contestant to complete a line wins.

Now consider the choices you have to make as producer.

VIEWING AUDIENCE

What audience is the programme aimed at?

▶ *Keep it as simple as the people in your group or a class in a local primary school. Whatever you choose, keep asking yourself, 'Would this audience find the programme understandable/entertaining?'*

BRANDING

▶ *What sort of quiz will it be? General knowledge, local knowledge, specialist (e.g. sport or pop music), zany?*

▶ *Give your programme a distinctive style through the name, the set design and logo. How can the title sequence help this process?*

▶ *How can the set or location suit the style of quiz? For instance, if you want a serious general knowledge quiz, you could simply use the library as your location. Alternatively, you might want to design and make a background that would be suited to a comedy quiz.*

PRESENTATION

▶ *Who will be the presenter and how will they be dressed? Do you want a male or female, someone serious or a 'character', a student or a teacher?*

▶ *How will you light your set? Will it be bright and cheerful or subdued and atmospheric?*

▶ *Do you want to add music or sound effects? If so, make sure they enhance the overall style and atmosphere you are aiming to create.*

▶ *How will you keep your camera steady? Think how you will frame your participants: will they all be in the picture together? Will the viewer be able to see the scoreboard? Who will mark the scoreboard? It is useful to make a **storyboard** or to write a script so that everyone involved knows what they have to do. Don't leave things to chance: plan ahead.*

STUDIO AUDIENCE

▶ *Will you have a 'studio audience'? If so, how do you want them to behave?*

PRODUCTION

▶ *If you have editing facilities, do you want to film the presenter, scoreboard and contestants separately using a single camera, then edit the programme later? Or do you want to use more than one camera and edit the different shots together?*

Do you want to add captions?

Evaluation

Using the discussion above, write an **evaluation** of the programme. Explain the following:

- the aims of your production
- how successfully you achieved these
- why your target audience was selected
- where you would schedule your production and why.

If a slightly longer evaluation is required, it could be organised like this:

Planning
The aim of the media text.
The audience that the text is aimed at.
Research (including market research) and planning undertaken.

Production
Use of technology and description of techniques.
How the audience was targeted.

Evaluation
Strengths and weaknesses of the media text.
Responses from audiences.
Proposed improvements and lessons learned.

Appendix
Any source material and evidence of planning.

Exam practice

Unseen moving image analysis

Record the openings (i.e. the first 2–3 minutes) of two contrasting quiz programmes.

- Read the questions below.
- Watch the extracts without making any notes.
- Watch them again, this time making notes that will help you to answer the questions.
- Watch the extracts twice more, each time making notes, then answer the questions, taking about an hour.

Questions

1 How are the two extracts typical of television quiz shows? Give reasons for your answer.

2 How do the openings try to attract the audience's interest? Consider:

   a music and sound effects
   b lighting
   c the role and personality of the presenter
   d the promise of rewards.

3 How are the contestants introduced and what is the relationship between the presenter and the contestants?

4 How does the set help to make the programmes more tense, interesting, exciting or lively?

Chapter 5

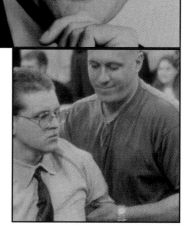

Television: talk shows

>> *This chapter covers:*

- how to analyse TV talk shows
- how to produce your own talk show
- exam practice on TV talk shows.

TV talk shows

Talk shows are cheap to produce because they use the same sets over and over again and the guests are free. Each programme focuses on a particular problem, which is related by members of the public and then discussed and examined by 'experts'. The programme usually has a helpline for people who are experiencing similar problems to those examined and who need advice.

Talk shows are different from **chat shows**, which tend to have celebrities talking about themselves in interviews.

Talk shows

- *Kilroy*
- *Esther*
- *Trisha*
- *The Oprah Winfrey Show*

Chat shows

- *Parkinson*
- *So Graham Norton*
- *The Frank Skinner Show*

Right: Trisha and guests
Far right: Kilroy

What sorts of programmes are talk shows? What are their conventions?

Working in pairs or small groups, make a list of programmes which you would call talk shows and discuss their similarities and differences.

▶ *Try to agree on a definition, but take note of any programmes that do not fit easily into the definition. Use the checklist below developed by media students to help with your discussion.*

Talk show conventions

- There is a host who is in control.
- The show is often named after the host, e.g. *Kilroy* and *Trisha*.
- There is a studio audience, whose members are asked to join in.
- There is usually a main problem or issue to be examined.

- There are members of the public whose problems are discussed.
- Sometimes experts are included to give their advice.
- The show is studio-based.
- Talk shows are usually screened during the daytime.
- They appeal to a mainly female audience.

Record and view extracts from two different talk shows and then use the questions and guidelines below to describe and analyse them.

SET DESIGN

*Set design is part of **mise-en-scène** (see page 14).*

Describe the relationship between the presenter, the audience and the guests.

▶ *What is the effect of having everyone together on the same level as opposed to having a stage?*

Above: Tempers flare during
The Jerry Springer Show

▶ *Often the audience is arranged in tiers to allow the cameras to focus on individuals. This arrangement suggests spectators at an event, and gives a different tone and atmosphere from having people grouped around a table or standing at a bar. Trisha tends to stay standing in the audience, but sometimes joins the guests and sits in one of the chairs 'on stage'.*

What is the effect of having a stage?

In *Kilroy* there is no stage, so does the audience at home feel as if it is joining in a casual discussion? Kilroy himself will sit amongst the studio audience, trying to give the impression that he is on the same level as everyone else.

STORIES

*What **stories** are there in the programmes? How are stories introduced? Summarise each story in fewer than 100 words.*

▶ *A common technique which you might find is the middle of a story being introduced. For example, at the start of the programme the host may say: 'Here is a woman whose husband is in jail for killing their son, but she believes he is innocent'. This leads the audience to want to know more: how did this situation arise? How did the story begin?*

*How does the programme present or encourage **complications** in stories?*

Find examples of the host saying something along the lines of: 'Let's go back to the beginning' or 'How did this come about?'

Look out for this being done by including in the audience a person with strong opinions who puts across an extreme point of view.

Look for examples of people involved in the story being introduced as the story develops.

*Find examples of **conflict** being encouraged:*

Host: *'Somebody over there said "disgusting".'* [Quick run with microphone across the studio.] *'Why did you say "disgusting"?'*

In Jerry Springer *fights frequently break out and guests have to be restrained by studio bouncers (see opposite).*

▶ *Look out for the use of **screen captions** that encourage a sense of expectation.*

In Trisha *on-screen captions provide such information as:*

'Backstage: The jealous husband waits to tell his side of the story.'

This caption is accompanied by an inset view of the husband waiting to be summoned. The word 'confront', suggesting conflict, is frequently emphasised on Trisha.

AUDIENCE REACTION

*Look out for examples of the **audience reacting** to statements made by the guests.*

▶ *There can be applause, usually when a member of the audience makes a point that many agree with. Sometimes there are gasps of astonishment to statements such as: 'She's just another notch on the bedpost.'*

THE ROLE OF THE HOST

Sometimes the host addresses the viewer directly and introduces the topic to be addressed. He/she introduces the people whose problems or conflicts are under discussion.

▸ Find examples of the host having **prior knowledge** of the experiences of the guests and leading the debate by talking them through their experiences. How does this give the host more authority or power?

▸ Look for examples of the host during the conflict stage being partly storyteller (or assistant storyteller) and partly inquisitor. For example, the host might say, 'Now, just a minute, what is the truth here? This isn't what you said at the start.'

▸ Find and describe examples of the host sometimes introducing invited **experts**, who are in the studio audience.

▸ Find and describe examples of the host acting as a **referee** in conflicts between guests.

CONTENT

*Identify the types of **problems** which are featured and those which are neglected.*

▸ To what extent does the programme focus on relationships, family feuds or personal problems?

▸ Does the programme try to find **solutions** to the problems examined?

The Trisha programme is not only a television show: it also works with a wide variety of organisations which help people with problems including The Samaritans, Childline and Victim Support. The Trisha website has fact-packs on topics such as:

▸ relationship difficulties caused by drugs and alcohol

▸ sexual problems

▸ eating disorders in teenagers and young adults.

Find instances of the programme seeking to present itself as a problem-solving service to viewers ('Let the Trisha team solve your family problems').

▸ Does the programme offer advice to viewers? ('Boys, if YOU don't want to be a dad, you know what to do …')

▸ How gender-biased is the programme? Are men generally represented as 'the problem' and women as victims?

▸ Find out what topics are currently highlighted on the Trisha website: www.angliatv.com/trisha

VIEWER INVOLVEMENT

*How are **the audience at home** encouraged to feel they are part of the show?*

Look at how the host works at this by using the inclusive 'we' in questions and statements: 'What we're all thinking is that …' or 'We all want to know why you did that'.

Find and describe examples of how the audience and viewers are encouraged to feel as if they are somehow helping to solve the problems of the guests.

How does the programme keep viewers interested and involved?

▶ Describe examples of people at home being encouraged to ring in with their problems:

> 'Revenge! Are you bursting with revenge? Has a lover or friend made you angry? So angry that you've maybe cut up their clothes? Or spent all their money? Maybe you've been the victim of a jealous rage. This is the number to ring...'

▶ Notice how the presenter might say, 'Well, maybe there is a way to talk this through. We'll find out after the break.'

▶ Find and describe examples of problems being simplified into a headline format which is superimposed on to the screen:

> 'You're a bad Dad'

> 'Women who stick by their men'

▶ Find and describe examples of how these are sometimes **updated** during the programme to highlight controversial developments:

> **'Katrina** – claims her ex, Shaun, is denying he's their son's dad!'
>
> **'Shaun** – claims she fell pregnant after a one-night stand!'
>
> **'Backstage**: Katrina's dad is not impressed with Shaun!'
>
> (Inset picture of father looking very aggressive)

▶ Look for statements and captions which arouse curiosity and **heighten anticipation**:

> 'Coming up: a daughter and dad meet for the first time!'

COMMERCIALS

What do the **commercials** tell you about the audience for the show?

On commercial television it is possible to tell what sort of audience the programme aims at by looking at the advertisements during the breaks. The following adverts were shown in one pre-Christmas break during a *Trisha* programme shown on Tyne Tees Television:

- a David Cassidy CD
- SCS sofas
- collectibles – 'classic pen set, the ideal gift'
- 'Increase your storage space with a loft conversion'
- 'Get rich this Christmas by winning on the National Lottery'
- Morrisons' superstore bargain buys
- Churchill car insurance

▸ *What does this list tell you about the gender, age and lifestyles of the* Trisha *audience?*

Produce your own talk show.

Your aim is to produce part of a talk show lasting a few minutes. You will need:

- a camcorder
- a space
- some helpers.

It would also be useful to have an extra camera, a tripod, some lighting equipment and an extra microphone, but these are not essential.

AUDIENCE

Keep your target audience as simple as the people in your group or a class in a local primary school. Keep asking yourself, 'Would this audience find the programme understandable and entertaining?'

▸ *Decide when the programme could be scheduled to reach this audience and on what channel.*

▸ *Give it a distinctive branding through the name, the set design and the programme logo.*

   Design a title sequence; make a set or choose a suitable location.

   Decide who will be the presenter and how he or she will be dressed.

   Think about lighting and camerawork.

CONTENT ISSUES

What sort of problem(s) will you discuss? Who will bring their problems to the programme? Will you bring in experts?

*Consider the issue of **privacy**. If you are discussing controversial topics, how will you protect the guests and people they mention from being offended or upset?*

Will you have an audience on the set? If so, how will you want them to behave?

*Write an **evaluation** of the programme, explaining briefly what your intentions were and to what extent you feel these intentions were fulfilled. What went wrong and why?*

(See chapter 6 for advice about camerawork. For advice about writing evaluations, see page 51.)

Exam practice ▬▬▬▬▬

Unseen moving image analysis

Record the first 2–3 minutes of two contrasting talk shows.

- ▪ Read the questions below.
- ▪ Watch the extracts without making any notes.
- ▪ Watch them again, this time making notes that will help you to answer the questions.
- ▪ Watch the extracts **twice** more, each time making notes, then answer the questions, choosing either an OCR board or a WJEC board format.

OCR board style

1 How are the two extracts typical of television talk shows? Give reasons for your answer.

2 How do the openings try to attract the audience's interest? Consider music and sound effects, lighting, the role and personality of the presenter and the hints of conflict.

3 How are the people with problems introduced, and what is the relationship between the presenter and these people?

4 Describe the sets. How might they influence the character of the programme?

WJEC board style

1 List three camera shots used in the extracts. Explain briefly why they have been used.

2 a Suggest a title for a new talk show aimed at teenagers.
 b Suggest a broadcast time and a channel for your programme.
 c Choose a host and give reasons for your choice.
 d Design a storyboard for your title sequence, identify key shots and select a soundtrack.
 e Give reasons why you think the programme will appeal to a teenage audience.

3 How is gender represented in the extracts you have viewed?

4 Explain why a talk show you have seen appeals to a television audience.

Chapter 6

Film comedy

>> *This chapter covers:*

- how to analyse comedy films
- case study of *Kind Hearts and Coronets*
- comparison of two successful film comedies
- information on *Carry On* films
- information on the role of independent cinemas
- pre-production exercises on producing a DVD cover, a publicity brochure for a programme of films and a poster for a comedy film.

READING THE MEDIA

Analysing film comedy

There are many kinds of comedy films, ranging from silent slapstick to satire and parody, from short cartoons to complex feature films. What they all have in common is a happy ending and the intention to make audiences laugh. Funny moments are basic to all comedy.

The fun, however, often has a serious purpose. Comedy is a way of laughing at things which need to be changed or challenged. These can be to do with how we behave, our habits and prejudices and our customs and beliefs. Alternatively, comedy can be about how the world is organised and controlled and how we can change the way we think or behave.

Jim Carrey in *The Mask*

Watch your favourite comedy film and then describe and analyse it using the questions and guidelines below.

*What **sorts of humour** does the film contain?*

Describe any examples of the following:

▸ **visual humour**, e.g. the custard pie in the face, trousers falling down, people falling over

▸ the **physical world letting characters down**, e.g. collapsing houses, runaway cars

▸ the **absurd**, as in cartoons, e.g. terrible things happen to characters' bodies, but they can become whole or normal again

▸ cruel or sarcastic verbal humour

▸ sexual innuendo

▸ quickfire witty wise-cracking

▸ self-criticism

▸ **satire**, which pokes fun at institutions or values

▸ **black comedy**, which takes serious subjects like death and war and makes jokes out of them for a serious purpose.

*How is the **story told** and who is the **storyteller**?*

> *Sometimes there is a **narrator** who tells the story, and the audience has to determine whether to trust or to doubt him or her.*

> *Sometimes there is an **all-seeing narrator** (the film director, if you like), who 'sees' things which the characters in the film are not aware of.*

*From whose **point of view** are the events shown?*

> ***Voice-overs**, where a character tells the story over the pictures, will affect how the audience interprets the story.*

> *The director can choose to have the camera show what the main character sees so that the audience can **identify** with him or her.*

> *The camera can also be **objective**, like a bystander, and this gives the audience more freedom to decide how to respond to events shown.*

In what order is the story told?

▸ *Do the events happen in chronological order or do we have **flashbacks** to the past and **flash forwards** to the future?*

*Most stories work from a problem or **inciting incident** (an event that triggers the story) through a series of **complications** to a satisfying **conclusion**, when order is restored.*

How many stories are there? Is there just one story or are there several?

▸ *Often there is a main story and a secondary story or sub-plot. Sometimes there are several stories woven together or linked – a **multiplot**.*

What sorts of **characters** are in the film?

▸ *Characters can be simple or complex. They can be typical, stereotypical or individual. They fill certain roles such as hero, heroine, villain, trickster, persecutor or victim.*

How are particular groups, classes and minorities **portrayed**?

▸ *When audiences laugh at something their laughter can be cruel or kind. Ask whether the humour is **destructive** or **constructive** and what is it attacking or asserting.*
▸ *We are often encouraged to laugh at **institutions** or **movements** which take themselves too seriously. Can you find an example of this?*
▸ *Sometimes we are encouraged to laugh at **social groups** (e.g. the English aristocracy in* Kind Hearts and Coronets*) or particular **races** (e.g. the British in* Austin Powers *movies), and that runs the risk of making us intolerant, encouraging prejudice. Is there any intolerance or prejudice in the film you are analysing?*

What is the **purpose** (if any) behind the comedy?

> *We can laugh at our own **weaknesses**, at the absurd things which humans do, and that can make us change the way we behave.*

> *Sometimes comedy can attack a **particular evil**, as in Chaplin's* The Great Dictator, *which ridiculed Hitler and Mussolini.*

Analysis of *Kind Hearts and Coronets*

This case study tries to show you how to apply the framework for study which is described at the beginning of this chapter to a particular film comedy.

A black comedy

In *Kind Hearts and Coronets*, an Ealing comedy made in 1949, the humour is mainly verbal. It is **black comedy** because it deals with the main character's successful attempts to murder those who stand in his way.

Each murder is cunningly plotted and coolly executed. Death is treated lightly and with humour from the start. We see the central character's father die rather theatrically, immediately after the birth of his son. The hero, Mazzini, played by Dennis Price, observes:

> 'My father succumbed to a heart attack the moment he set eyes on me.'

Mazzini's first crime is to dispose of Ascoyne d'Ascoyne (the names are meant to sound ridiculous). Mazzini unties the boat in which his victim and the woman with whom he has spent the weekend are embracing, and it is swept over a dangerous weir. The event is partly humorous because it looks so unlikely and absurd. Then Mazzini says quite calmly as the couple disappear:

> 'I felt sorry for the girl, but found some consolation in the reflection that she had presumably at some stage during the weekend undergone a fate worse than death.'

Usually, however, it is Mazzini's cruel humour that we see. When he fires an arrow to burst Lady Agatha's balloon as she glides above London dropping leaflets about the suffragette movement, he says:

> 'I shot an arrow in the air. She fell to earth in Berkeley Square.'

The **way the murders are filmed** accentuates the humour, and the **camera positions** are particularly important here. We tend to see things either from a distance or in long shot.

When the rowing boat goes over the weir, it is in long shot. We do not see the victims, nor hear their cries, nor see their struggles to survive. Such scenes, which would be appropriate in a thriller, have no place in a comedy. In fact, there is very little use of close-ups at all, so that the audience does not become emotionally involved with the victims. That would destroy the humour.

Story and point of view

The main character and storyteller is Louis Mazzini and the film is about his search for revenge. His rich relatives rejected his mother, a duke's daughter, because she married a penniless opera singer. Mazzini decides to murder his way to the title which he thinks he has been robbed of.

The way the story is told helps the black humour to work. We see things from Mazzini's point of view. We identify with him and like him not only because he is cool and stylish, but also because he is fighting for fair play in a cruel society. The problem is that he is committing crimes in order to do this – but then, sympathising with lawbreakers is not an unusual position for audiences to take.

The film-makers seem to want you to like Mazzini, as so much is presented from his point of view. It is reluctantly that they have him make the mistake of leaving his diary in prison, which will probably lead to his execution. Basically, he is portrayed as a competent, intelligent and likeable rogue.

Narrative sequence

The film is one long **flashback**. This makes the audience curious. We know that this man is about to be executed, but we don't know what he has done. As the murders are depicted through the course of the film, we begin to wonder how Mazzini was caught when everything seems to be going so smoothly. Then, near the ending of the film, there are several **twists** that surprise us so that our attention is engaged right up to the last frame.

Dennis Price as Louis Mazzini in
Kind Hearts and Coronets

Portrayal of social groups

The **targets of the humour** are the British class system and the coldness and hypocrisy of aristocratic values. The d'Ascoynes are arrogant and harsh, treating the lower classes with disdain. For example, Ascoyne d'Ascoyne has Mazzini dismissed for answering him back in the drapery store and Ethelred sets illegal mantraps for poachers, who are then beaten by his game-keeper. As Mazzini kills him, he says, 'I swore to have my revenge on your intolerable pride.'

The two main female characters in the film, Sibella and Edith, seem at first to be **portrayals of women** verging on the **stereotypical**. They represent two common masculine ideas about females: the flirtatious temptress (Sibella) and the stern mother figure (Edith). However, there is more to Sibella than meets the eye: she is the only person to see through Mazzini's scheming.

Character portrayal

The aristocratic characters, who are all played by the same actor, are not complex. They are briefly and simply drawn. We do not see events from their point of view. This means that we do not develop any sympathy for them or their class.

Comic purpose

The film is a **comment on its times** because it represented a rebellious state-ment against the upper classes in Britain. It was made in 1949, after the Second World War and the landslide victory of a Labour government. There was an atmosphere of social change and less respect for traditional authority.

There are hints in the film of **women playing more forceful roles**. This was a result of the confidence that the war gave to many women because they had to do 'men's work' while the men were in the forces.

Another target of the humour is the way some lower-class people give **too much respect** to the aristocracy. The executioner at the beginning of the film is an example. He is terribly concerned about how he should address a duke and he practises bowing. He also announces that after this execution he will retire because after using a silken rope he could 'never again be content with hemp'.

Audience reaction

Audiences will **interpret** the film in different ways. Some people will find the portrayal of the landed gentry too simple and think that the attacks on their atti-tudes and values are unfair.

Others will share Mazzini's disapproval of the snobbery of the upper class. They may admire his ingenuity and his cool composure. However, some people may consider him a heartless upstart who deserves to be sent to jail.

Ealing Studios

Kind Hearts and *Coronets* was one of a series of films produced by Ealing Studios in London just after the Second World War.
The others include:

- *Hue and Cry*
  (Charles Crichton, 1947)
- *Passport to Pimlico*
  (Henry Cornelius, 1949)
- *Whisky Galore!*
  (Alexander Mackendrick, 1951)
- *The Lavender Hill Mob*
  (Charles Crichton, 1951)
- *The Man in the White Suit*
  (Alexander Mackendrick, 1951)
- *The Ladykillers*
  (Alexander Mackendrick, 1951)
- *The Titfield Thunderbolt*
  (Charles Crichton, 1953).

The studios produced on average five films per year. The films were all U-certificate (i.e. suitable for audiences of all ages), lasting for about an hour and a half and costing £200,000 or less to produce. They were distributed by J. Arthur Rank Ltd, which owned the Odeon and Gaumont cinema chains.

Rank agreed to show all Ealing films as top-of-the-bill attractions. Each film took about 10 weeks to shoot. This works out at two minutes' screen time for every day of filming.

The films were characterised by bland lighting, static camerawork, little or no atmospheric music, few locations and an emphasis on dialogue.

Woody Allen, director and star of *Small Time Crooks*

Compare and contrast *Small Time Crooks* and *Kind Hearts and Coronets*.

These two films make a good contrast because they are from different periods and cultures, and have very different technical qualities.

Compare the sequence in Kind Hearts and Coronets *(UK 1949) where Louis Mazzini kills Lady Agatha (the suffragette) with the sequence in* Small Time Crooks *(USA 2000) in which Woody Allen and his helpers try to tunnel through to the bank.*

▸ *What features of these extracts identify them as comedies?*

▸ *What do you learn about the characters through dialogue, costume and actions – i.e. the **mise-en-scène** (see page 14)?*

▸ *Consider camerawork, set design, acting quality, lighting, editing and sound. What differences are there between the two sequences in terms of production values?*

▸ *Notice how both films are about crimes and about people trying to improve their social status.*

▸ *Explain the twists at the end of each film.*

▸ *How are women represented in the films?*

▸ *Describe how the upper classes are portrayed in the two films. In particular, look at behaviour, pastimes, values, snobbery and hypocrisy.*

The *Carry On* films

The *Carry On* series of British comedy films began in 1958. There are 31 films in all. Each contains saucy humour, sexual innuendo, larger-than-life characters, slapstick humour and appalling puns ('Infamy! Infamy! They've all got it in for me!' – Kenneth Williams as Julius Caesar).

Great emphasis is placed on **double meanings**, but there is never any coarse language or open sexuality. As Charles Hawtrey, a veteran *Carry On* actor, observed: 'I do not object to jiggery, but I do take exception to pokery.'

With their irreverent humour, *Carry On* films **poke fun at British institutions**, including the army, police, health service and education system. They also **parody film genres** such as the western, horror and James Bond films.

The stories follow a **standard pattern**. The order of an institution (e.g. the army, a hospital or police force) is disrupted by a series of comic **complications** and misunderstandings, bringing near chaos before some **resolution** at the end of the film.

The **characters are always the same** whatever the story. Kenneth Williams is aloof, camp and effeminate; Sid James, crude and lecherous; Charles Hawtrey, a hapless innocent, constantly being caught with his trousers down.

The characters were usually **stereotypes**: the gay fool, the battleaxe, the busty glamour girl, the nagging wife, etc.

Further study
A study of the films listed below would enable you to look at portrayal of gender and social class, attacks on institutions (army and health service) and the use of historical setting and costume:

- *Carry On Sergeant* (1958)
- *Carry On Nurse* (1959)
- *Carry On Cabby* (1963)
- *Carry On Cleo* (1964).

The role of independent cinema

Independent cinemas differ from multiplexes in terms of the films they screen, the audiences they attract and their general atmosphere. Although some of the films they show are commercially popular, especially if the independent cinema is privately owned, most are aimed at a minority audience.

In order to qualify for grants from the British Film Institute and other forms of public subsidy, independents need to show that they are meeting a demand not catered for by the main cinema chains.

The films shown in multiplexes are mainly the latest Hollywood blockbusters. They are shown as long as they are attracting audiences and making a profit. In independent cinemas, programmes may be determined months in advance and often focus on particular themes, such as the work of a particular director or films from a single foreign country. Independents are more likely to show classic films from the past, short films, documentaries, subtitled films and experimental films.

The atmosphere of an independent cinema is also different from a multiplex. Instead of popcorn and hot-dog stands there will be a coffee bar and often a shop selling film-related merchandise. The cinema itself will be small and possibly part of a larger venue such as an arts centre.

Independent UK cinemas supported by the British Film Institute

■ EAST
Aldeburgh Cinema
Cinema City (Norwich)
Ipswich Film Theatre

■ LONDON
Barbican (EC2)
Institute of Contemporary Arts (SW1)
Lux Cinema (N1)
Rio Cinema (E8)
Riverside Studios(W6)
Watermans (Brentford)

■ HOME COUNTIES
Campus West (Welwyn Garden City)
Reading Film Theatre

■ MIDLANDS
Broadway in Nottingham Media Centre
Cinema in the Square (Shrewsbury)
Forum Cinema (Northampton)
Lighthouse (Wolverhampton)
MAC (Birmingham)
Metro Cinema (Derby)
Phoenix Arts (Leicester)
Stoke Film Theatre
Warwick Arts Centre (Coventry)

■ NORTH EAST AND YORKSHIRE
The Arc (Stockton)
Hull Screen
Pictureville (Bradford)
The Showroom (Sheffield)

■ NORTH EAST AND YORKSHIRE (contd)
The Tyneside Cinema (Newcastle)
York Film Theatre

■ NORTH WEST
The Brewery (Kendal)
Cornerhouse (Manchester)
Crosby Community Centre (Liverpool)
The Dukes (Lancaster)

■ NORTHERN IRELAND
Queens Film Theatre (Belfast)

■ SOUTH EAST AND SOUTH
Brighton Cinemathèque
Cinema 3 (Canterbury)
The Gantry(Southampton)
New Park Cinema (Chichester)

■ SOUTH WEST
Plymouth Arts Centre
The Barn Theatre (Totnes)
The Guildhall Arts Centre (Gloucester)
The Strode Theatre (Somerset)
The Watershed (Bristol)

■ WALES
Chapter (Cardiff)
Taliesin Arts Centre (Swansea)
Theatr Clwyd (Mold)
Theatr Mwldan (Cardigan)
The Coliseum (Aberdare)

Design a DVD cover.

Choose a comedy film that you know. Imagine that it is being released on DVD as part of a series on British Comedy. It is expected to appeal to film buffs and people interested in the comedy genre. Design a cover and draw up a list of extra contents that might be attractive to the target audience.

Your cover could include:

- *the title*
- *the director's name, the film's year of release and country of origin*
- *running time*
- *whether the film is in colour or black and white*
- *names of stars*
- *soundtrack details*
- *comments from critics.*

Possible DVD extras could include:

- *clips from principal actors' other films*
- *interviews with the cast, director and critics*
- *background information about the production and the studio*
- *clips from similar films*
- *contemporary advertising materials, such as posters*
- *the trailer*
- *alternative endings.*

Design a poster for a comedy film.

Produce a film poster advertising a comedy film.

You will need to:

- *make up a title*
- *decide what sort of comedy (e.g. slapstick, romantic, satirical) your film will contain*
- *decide what audience it is aimed at*
- *decide what that audience will expect from the film*
- *write a sentence or some phrases about the comedy which will arouse people's interest or curiosity*
- *name the stars the film will have and find pictures of the actors which you can use/adapt*
- *include some critics' opinions*
- *make sure that there is one dominant visual image*
  make sure that the print is big enough to be read from a distance.

COMICAL CROOKS

Gormless gangsters!

Incompetent kidnappers!

Bungling burglars!

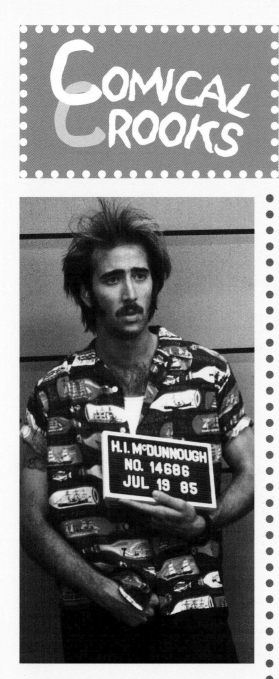

Nicholas Cage in the Coen Brothers' cult comedy classic
Raising Arizona

CASE 1
Tuesday 21st August

RAISING ARIZONA

Dir. Joel Coen USA 1987 94 mins.

Nicholas Cage is at his best as the incompetent robber who marries a prison officer. Unable to produce children of their own, the couple kidnap one of the famous Arizona quintuplets. Complications occur when two of Cage's old cellmates turn up looking for sanctuary – and things get nasty when the the baby's father hires a sinister biker to find his child…

'Hilarious' *Time Out*

CASE 2
Thursday 23rd and Friday 24th August

THE LADYKILLERS

Dir. Alexander Mackendrick GB 97 mins.
An old lady plays innocent hostess to a gang of robbers posing as musicians. She unwittingly foils a getaway and the gang hilariously bump each other off, leaving her with the proceeds of the crime.

'A delight' *EMPIRE*

CASE 3
Monday 27th to Thursday 30th August

SMALL TIME CROOKS (15)

Dir. Woody Allen USA 95 mins
Allen is a none-too-bright petty crook who leads a gang of dim low-lifes in a plot to rob a bank. The plot fails, but Allen's wife (Tracey Ullman) becomes rich through the cookie shop she starts as a cover. This only brings complications as she tries to improve herself socially and culturally while Allen longs for the simple life…

'Ullman is brilliant' *UNCUT*

Compile a history of cinemas in your area.

▸ *Find out how many cinemas there were before television became popular in the mid-to-late 1950s and produce a map to show where these were.*

▸ *Try to find out what audiences were like and how different cinema-going was from the present day by interviewing local people with clear memories.*

▸ *To start people reminiscing, you could ask about queuing, B-movies, double seats in the back row, and Saturday morning film clubs.*

▸ *Compare the locations and numbers of cinemas with what these are today.*

▸ *What has happened to the buildings which used to be cinemas?*

Compile a programme of films for a local independent cinema.

Choose three or four films which will appeal to regular filmgoers with a special interest in film history and/or comedy or science fiction. One part of the programme should be dedicated to the development of film comedy or science fiction. You could show the development by having films from different decades. Alternatively, you could choose a theme such as the portrayal of aliens in science fiction films or comedies about crime.

Write briefly *about each film you select and write a short introduction to the programme.*

An example is shown on page 69.

PRACTICAL FILMING

See the activities on pages 82–87 of Chapter 7.

Science fiction films

>> *This chapter covers:*

- how to analyse a science fiction film
- description and analysis of *Galaxy Quest*
- information on film genres
- Hollywood, the studio system and after
- the costs of film-making
- how a film is marketed
- suggestions for your own practical productions
- advice on filming techniques.

READING THE MEDIA

Analysing science fiction films

It should be fairly easy to tell the difference between a science fiction film and, for example, a western or a musical – though some people have described *Star Wars* as a western. But the distinction between some science fiction films and, say, some thrillers or fantasy films is not always clear. In fact, the science fiction genre is often broken down by critics into different types of sci-fi, which are called **sub-genres**. These include:

- 'end of the world'
- threatening alien invasions
- friendly alien invasions
- alien invasions by stealth
- nuclear threats
- mutations of earth creatures created by bad science
- prophecy.

In small discussion groups, try to sort the classic sci-fi films below into the main sci-fi sub-genres.

Classic sci-fi films

- *Things to Come* (1936)
  Based on a story by H.G. Wells, this depicted a long and futile war followed by a plague, the Wandering Sickness. The remains of a devastated world are ruled over by a cruel Boss who orders that plague victims be shot on sight. He himself is killed (with 'Peace Gas') by John Cabal, who descends from the skies. He comes from Wings Over the World and warns Earth to make peace or die.

- *Seven Days to Noon* (1950)
  A British film about a professor so worried about the potential use of the atomic bomb he has been working on that he threatens to blow up London unless further experiments are halted. In a classic suspense formula, he is stopped just before the protest bomb explodes.

- The *Quatermass* films (late 1950s)
  These can be read either as a comment on Britain's decline as an international power facing unknown forces or as a reference to the anti-nuclear debate.

Above: Mad scientist Richard Attenborough in *Jurassic Park*

- *The Beast From 20,000 Fathoms* (1953), *Them* (1954), *It Came From Beneath the Sea* (1955), *The Amazing Colossal Man* (1957), and *The Most Dangerous Man Alive* (1961)
  All these films were produced at a time when both the United States and Britain were testing nuclear weapons and people were concerned about the possible effects. These effects were usually depicted as various kinds of mutations.

- *The War of the Worlds* (1953)
  Reptilian Martians blast Earth to near-submission.

- *The Thing From Another World* (1951)
  An invading force consisting of a single but very dangerous vegetable creature is at large in the Antarctic.

- *The Day The Earth Stood Still* (1951)
  A space visitor named Klaatu comes to Earth from a kind of interstellar United Nations with a message of non-violence. He is greeted with panic and aggression. He lands his spaceship on the White House lawn and says that he comes in peace, but when he goes to take a gift from inside his tunic a jittery soldier shoots and wounds him. It turns out that other planets are worried about Earth's liking for violence and that once atomic power has been mastered our planet will pose a threat to other galaxies. 'If you threaten to extend your violence, this Earth of yours will be reduced to a cinder,' Klaatu warns near the end of the film.

Sci-fi sub-genres

- [ ] 'end of the world'
- [ ] threatening alien invasions
- [ ] friendly alien invasions
- [ ] alien invasions by stealth
- [ ] nuclear threats
- [ ] mutations of earth creatures created by bad science
- [ ] prophecy

- *Invasion of the Body Snatchers* (1956)
  The invaders use brain-embedded devices to turn ordinary people into destructive zombies. At the time this film was made, alien forces were often meant to represent communism in America.

- *Them* (1954)
  Giant ants created by nuclear mishap attack Los Angeles.

- *The Beginning of the End* (1957)
  Giant grasshoppers, created by nuclear mishap, threaten Chicago.

- *Jurassic Park* (1993)
  The cloning of dinosaurs from the blood of insects preserved in amber goes badly wrong and humans are attacked by the resulting monsters.

- *Independence Day* (1996)
  This is a story of the extra-terrestrial invasion of the world, beginning with the destruction of the White House, with spectacular effects including mile-wide spaceships attacking Earth's major cities. Can be compared with *War of the Worlds*.

- *Minority Report* (2002)
  Using 'Precogs' or people who can see into the future, police have mastered the ability to predict crimes of violence and can arrest people before they commit a crime.

Above: Publicity still from the apocalyptic sci-fi blockbuster *Independence Day*

Choose a science fiction film and describe and analyse it using the following questions and guidelines.

Technical effects
What special technical effects are there? How realistic are the monsters and the space vehicles? In particular, look at illusions of space, time travel, planets, size and speed.

Story
*What **type of story** does the film tell? Is it about alien invasion, a mad scientist, environmental disaster, space travel, nuclear havoc?*

*From whose **point of view** is the story told? Are the events told in the same order in which they happen or are there any flashbacks or flash-forwards in time? How does the film begin and end?*

Characters
What roles do the characters play? Are there established and particular roles such as heroes, villains, victims, helpers, magicians etc?

Topical concerns
*How does the film reflect **topical concerns** and issues? For example, does it reflect any worries about the environment, about dangers from space, or about biological and chemical warfare?*

*What **conflicts** does the film explore and how are they **resolved**?*

*How are different individuals, groups, and occupations **portrayed**?*

Are scientists portrayed as dangerous or helpful? Are villains associated with particular countries or movements?

*What **oppositions** are shown, e.g. science v nature, good v evil, West v East, pacifism v warmongering, greed v generosity?*

Suggest different interpretations for the film.

▸ *Try to identify the intended message(s) of the film and suggest other interpretations. For example, some American films suggest that national pride and harmony make the country stronger, but it can be argued that they encourage triumphalism, which makes the USA more detested by some groups and therefore more vulnerable to attack.*

Audience involvement
How does the film try to keep the audience involved? Is there suspense? Are there surprises or twists in the story?

Does the film try to excite, thrill, shock, change people's attitudes or argue a particular case?

*Does the film attract large followings of **fans**?*

▸ *Look for examples of **fan clubs** and **merchandise** associated with particular series of films. Star Wars is a particularly good example to study. Does the film which you are studying have a fan club or generate merchandise such as clothing or toys?*

Description and analysis of *Galaxy Quest* (USA 1999, dir. Dean Parisot)

This case study shows how the questions above can be applied to the analysis of a particular film.

To which sci-fi sub-genre does the film belong?
This spoof science fiction film is a take-off of the television sci-fi series *Star Trek*. It features both dangerous and friendly aliens, and adventures in space including visits to new planets.

It provides both **comedy and excitement**. Jason Nesmith (Tim Allen), Gwen De Marco (Sigourney Weaver), Alexander Dane (Alan Rickman), Fred Kwan (Tony Shalout), Guy Fleegman (Sam Rockwell), and Tommy Webber (Daryl Mitchell) are actors who play the main parts in a television series called *Galaxy Quest*, which closely resembles *Star Trek*. They attend a convention packed with fans of the show.

Attending the convention are Thermian aliens, who at first are assumed to be fans in fancy dress. But these aliens have come for help. They have seen the *Galaxy Quest* shows and think that they are real-life not fiction. They transport Jason to their spaceship, which has been constructed as a replica of the one on the TV show, and ask him to fight off the evil Sarris. Jason fetches the others from Earth to join him on the spaceship and together they take on the evil aliens and destroy them.

A scene from
the spoof sci-fi film
Galaxy Quest

The humour comes from watching actors suddenly transported from their pretend world into a 'real' fantasy, where they try desperately to recreate the bravery and skill that they usually exhibit in the television series. They return to earth in a spaceship crashing, conveniently, into another *Galaxy Quest* convention.

Point of view

The story is told mainly from the **point of view** of Jason Nesmith, who plays the commander in *Galaxy Quest*. Once he has been transported to the spaceship in a process that parodies 'beam me up, Scotty' in *Star Trek*, the narrative is a series of mini-adventures during which the crew have to combat various crises.

Conflicts and oppositions

The **conflicts** are the **stock types** of TV science fiction:

- the evil aliens attack in their spaceship
- there is a chase through space
- a space minefield is encountered
- the spaceship runs out of fuel
- the characters have to land on a planet to find some new supplies – *'Captain, we've found some beryllium on a nearby planet'*
- the planet turns out to be inhospitable and the crew have to run to escape some ferocious miniature aliens
- the captain is stranded and attacked first by a pig lizard, which is all mouth and hardly any legs, and then by a monster made out of rocks
- the 'digital conveyer' comes to his rescue, transporting him instantaneously through space back to the ship
- when Sarris and his followers transport themselves into the Thermian spaceship, there is a series of chases and fights in different parts of the ship.

There is also the matter of an 'implosion missile', which is set to blow up the spaceship. There is a chance of stopping it but there is a time limit. We see the countdown on a digital clock which miraculously stops just before zero. Gwen De Marco observes: 'It always stops at one on the show.'

What roles do the characters play?

The main **characters** are based on the *Star Trek* characters. Jason is like Captain Kirk, full of noble sentiments and brave aphorisms, e.g. 'Never give up and never surrender.' He is also very vain, keen to take his shirt off in a fight to display his physique. He persists in diving to the ground and firing his gun unnecessarily when on a strange planet.

Gwen De Marco (Weaver) is the token Uhuru character who repeats what computers say and flaunts her cleavage. Dr Lazarus (Rickman) is the Spock character who, instead of having pointy ears, has what looks like half an octopus on his head. Fred Kwan is a slow-talking version of Scotty the *Star Trek* engineer, who says technical-sounding things which are meaningless.

Portrayal of individuals, groups and occupations

There is quite a range of **aliens**. The good ones, Thermians, resemble human beings – or at least they do when they carry out their 'appearance change'. Ordinarily, they look like octopuses. They have strange voices and fixed smiles which make them 'other-worldly' and zombie-like, but they are gentle, trusting souls at heart.

Not so Sarris and his kin. Sarris is a large lobster-like figure who enjoys torturing people: 'There will be blood and pain as you cannot imagine!' At least you know where you stand with an evil-looking monster. But the little miners on the strange planet look gentle and kind, not the type at all to ask of the captured commander, 'What shall we do with him?' and to answer, 'Hit him on the head and eat him.'

The aliens are all convincingly constructed, with slight touches of silliness to make them amusing. Sarris's spiny 'hair' and his eye-patch stop him being completely repulsive, while the Thermians' white complexions, severe hair-styles and computer-like voices are strange enough to make them alien but not bizarre enough to alienate the audience. The spaceships are convincing models and their powers of acceleration and ability to travel through 'black holes' are sufficiently over-the-top to be funny without seeming ridiculous.

Treatment of topical issues

The film is basically a gentle **satire** on predictable TV science fiction, but it also attacks people who take TV too seriously and attend conventions, dressing like the screen characters and parroting the meaningless phrases of the characters.

The film also takes a gentle swipe at the actors who play these parts and make commercial success out of their stardom by pretending to be enthusiastic but under the surface despising what they do.

Audience involvement

The film is a satire, but the satire does not work unless the **audience** are familiar not only with the television science fiction series *Star Trek* but also with 'Trekkies' – people who are passionate fans of the programme. The audience are positioned by the film's humour and points of view to laugh at the conventions of *Star Trek* and the excesses of its followers.

Film genres

Genres are types of film (see page 2). They are produced by the **interaction of the film studios and the mass audience**, and they survive as long as they satisfy the needs and expectations of the audience. They are recognised by people who watch films and by film-makers themselves. Producers need to know what kinds of films sell and audiences need to know what to expect when they go to the cinema.

Examples of film genres include:

- musical
- crime
- western
- horror
- science fiction
- action/adventure
- melodrama
- comedy
- thriller
- teenpic.

In any genre, the **stories** are predictable and the **settings** familiar. The plots develop through conventional **conflicts** to a predictable ending. Familiar characters perform familiar actions which celebrate familiar values.

There has to be some **degree of variation** to keep audiences interested. The producers of the films have to balance predictability and novelty.

The audience learns to understand certain images and sounds so that, for instance, the white hat and white horse in a traditional western tell us we are seeing a hero, while a bunch of men dressed in overcoats and trilby hats and carrying what look like musical instruments as they emerge from a 1920s saloon car signals 'gangsters'.

The studio system

The **studio system** refers to the practices of film-making from 1930 to 1960 in Hollywood which are similar to the **production line in a factory**.

The major studios in those times, MGM, Twentieth Century Fox, Warner Brothers, Paramount and RKO, made pictures and leased them through their own distribution companies to cinemas which they themselves owned.

By attending cinemas in huge numbers during these years, audiences encouraged the **mass distribution of films**. To some extent, they also determined the format of the films themselves. Audiences' preferences for particular stories and techniques led to **repetition**, and certain cinematic conventions became established.

The relationship worked both ways. There was a **huge demand** for films during this period, as the majority of the population went to the cinema. The average attendance was twice a week. Each programme consisted of an **A** (main) film and a **B** (support) film. At its peak, the Hollywood studio system was producing between 400 and 700 films per year.

This huge demand led to a **division of labour**, where people concentrated on one small job rather than lots of jobs. This meant that people became **specialists**. Actors became proficient at certain types of role, scriptwriters developed talents for different sorts of stories and directors specialised in certain styles of film.

The costs of making a film could be kept down by **repeating successful formulas**. For instance, certain sorts of sets, costumes and props were repeatedly used. It is worth remembering that some B films were completed in as little as a fortnight from scripting to editing. This left little room for innovation.

The system led to each major studio developing its **own style** of film. For example, MGM went in for large-budget costume drama and musicals such as *The Wizard of Oz* (1939), whereas Warner Bros. specialised in gangster films such as *Little Caesar* (1930).

Warner's average cost of production in 1932 was $200,000 per feature compared with MGM's $450,000. This meant, among other things, that the sets on Warner films were comparatively inexpensive and one consequence of this was that low-key lighting was used to disguise their cheapness.

The system was challenged in 1948 by the **Paramount Decree**, by which the American Supreme Court forced the big studios to sell off their theatres so that they no longer controlled the whole process of making, distributing and showing their films. It also prevented them from having an active involvement with television.

The studio system was also weakened by the **decline of cinema-going** caused by the growing popularity of television. Film production became more 'one-off' than 'assembly line' with independent production companies.

Changes in Hollywood

In the 1950s and early 60s Hollywood studios went through a difficult period, producing a run of pictures, mainly musicals, which were costly flops. This was partly because studio bosses failed to spot the emergence of a sophisticated new **youth audience**, which made hits of films with anti-heroes, such as:

- *The Graduate* (1967)
- *Bonnie and Clyde* (1967)
- *Easy Rider* (1969)
- *Butch Cassidy and the Sundance Kid* (1969)
- *Midnight Cowboy* (1969).

A **new breed of directors** emerged. Directors such as Martin Scorsese, Francis Coppola and George Lucas had been educated at film schools and were interested in the techniques of European film-makers such as François Truffaut and Jean-Luc Godard.

This led to the **main characters** being less sure of themselves, more mysterious or contradictory and the stories becoming more open-ended. The main characters no longer achieved their goals of solving a case, or getting the woman, or clearing someone's name.

Case Study
Film finance

The cost of making a film depends on whether:

- it is made by a big-budget studio or a low-budget indie company
- there are stars in it
- it is in a modern setting or set in the past
- it involves expensive special effects.

However, it is still possible to make some general points about how much a movie will cost to make and what returns can be expected over the film's lifetime.

In 2000, the average cost of making a Hollywood studio movie up to the production of the negative was $54.8 million. That did not include the making of show prints (about $1,000 each) and advertising. For a low-budget indie film, the cost is more like $20 million.

The costs of **prints and advertising** on average are $10 million for indies and $27 million for the big budget movies. The negative cost (cost up to producing a negative) of *Titanic* was $200 million.

Production costs
Production costs are divided into **above the line** and **below the line**.

- **Above the line** means the talent: the actors, the writers, the director, the producers
- **Below the line** is everything else: the crew, the sets, the costumes, food, transport, and so on, and the post-production costs of editing, sound, music, etc.

Stars can be expensive. A top leading man like Harrison Ford or Tom Cruise can cost $25 million, plus a percentage of the income. Leading ladies are less expensive – Meg Ryan or Sigourney Weaver would demand about $15 million. Rising young stars such as Freddie Prinz Jnr or Katie Holmes would cost approximately $2 million. Not all of that payment goes to the actors themselves: most stars employ an entourage of professionals such as stylists, trainers, caterers, acting coaches, drug counsellors, and so on.

Actors with speaking parts cost $617 per day for big-budget films and $466 for low budgets, while extras earn $100 per day. A top director will earn $3 million, plus a percentage of profits.

Other costs include:

make-up artists and stylists	
set designer	$42 per hour
senior illustrator (producing storyboards) (The *Batman* movies had 20 such illustrators.)	$1,258 per week $1,752 per week
art directors (say, three per film)	
gaffers (chief lighting technicians)	$2,503 per week
electricians (say, 30 per film)	$31 per hour
picture editor	$27 per hour
sound editor	$1,628 per week $1,628 per week

Earnings
Earnings come from box offices, video sales and rentals, and television rights. Here are the estimated takings for *My Best Friend's Wedding* (1997), which starred Julia Roberts and cost an estimated $73 million to make:

share of United States box office	$63.4 million
share of world box office take	$111 million
video sales and rentals	$58.5 million
TV broadcast rights	$15 million
	Total $248.1 million
	Profit $175.1 million

Still from the opening scene
of Spielberg's *Jaws*

The release of Spielberg's *Jaws* in 1975 marked another important turning point. Heavily advertised prior to its launch, it opened in cinemas all over America and grossed $48 million in its first three days.

Jaws marked the birth of the **blockbuster film**. Rather than have its studios producing steady series of films which made a modest financial return, Hollywood began producing expensive one-offs which could make massive profits. Blockbuster films became multi-purpose **entertainment machines** with videos, soundtrack albums, video games, theme-park rides and comic books.

The huge profits which blockbusters could make can be seen in the success of *Star Wars*, which cost $11 million to make and within three years had earned over $500 million.

Marketing a film

The information cascade

Film audiences make hits or flops, and they do it not by revealing preferences but by discovering what they like. Because they do not know for sure what a film will be like until they have seen it, they rely on information from **friends and reviewers** before deciding whether to go and see it. This is why it is difficult to predict how well a movie will do. Whether or not it succeeds partly depends on what the first viewers tell their friends about it.

Film distributors have to **get people talking** about a film. They can do this by investing a lot of cash in initial publicity. If you attract a large number of people into the cinema you start an **information cascade**.

Sometimes, distributors will invite audiences to **previews** to start the cascade. Taxi drivers and hairdressers are favourite preview audiences because both groups talk to large numbers of the public. Distributors also use test audiences to gauge a film's likely success. Some films are completed but never shown if test audiences do not like them.

MAKING THE MEDIA

Design a poster for a sci-fi film

Use the picture below or one of your own to produce a film poster advertising a science fiction film. You will need to:

▸ make up a title
▸ decide what sub-genre your film is
▸ name your stars
▸ write a sentence or some phrases about the story to arouse interest or curiosity
▸ include some critics' opinions
▸ select a dominant visual image from the film
▸ make sure that the print is big enough to read from a distance.

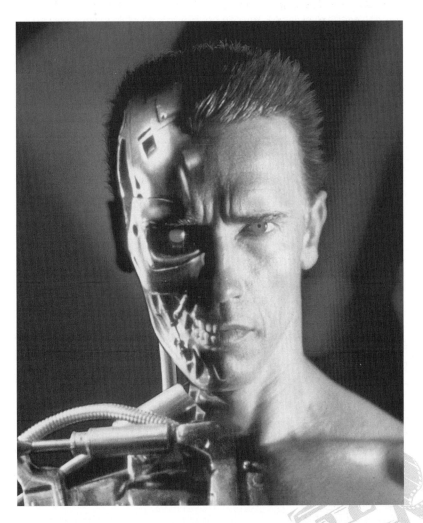

Arnold Schwarzenegger in
Terminator 2

Before making a short film, practise your filming skills as follows:

▸ *Study the techniques described on pages 84–85.*
▸ *Take different types of shot as illustrated below until you get used to holding a camera steady.*
▸ *In each case hold the camera still, using a tripod if necessary.*
▸ *Look carefully at the results and think about **lighting sources**.
Are the subjects you were filming lit the way you want? If not, can the lighting be improved by changing the camera position or introducing artificial lighting?*

It is best to film in the early morning or after rain if you are filming outside. Avoid filming into the sun or with the sun directly behind you. If filming Inside, you can use borrowed lights from the drama department or anglepoise desk lamps. You can bounce light off white surfaces or use reflectors made out of polystyrene or aluminium foil.

Try experimenting with different lighting set-ups until you get it right.

▸ *Think about composition. The natural thing to do if you are just beginning to film is to place the subject in the centre of the frame, but sometimes better results can be achieved by filming the subject slightly off-centre.*

▸ *Think about backgrounds. Is there anything in the backgrounds of your shots that distracts from the subject?*

Now try filming the same sequence of shots, this time improving their quality.

▸ *You can also try to film one subject from **three angles**:*

    – *by standing on a table or chair and pointing the camera down*
    – *by standing at the same level and pointing the camera straight*
    – *by lying on the floor and pointing the camera upwards.*

When you look at these shots later, try to work out how the different angles make you see something differently.

Film a 2-3 minute scene from a comedy of your own devising.

Here are some examples to get you thinking:

▸ *A comic **props** scene where everyday objects start behaving strangely, such as a photocopier that delivers hamburgers and squirts ketchup
An **escalation** scene where actions and reactions become more and more bizarre. For example, a student scribbles on another's work; the second student retaliates by tearing the other's work into pieces, whereupon the first tips the contents of the other's bag over the floor – and so on*

- ▸ *Incongruous situations*, such as a short-sighted driving instructor telling someone how to start a car
- ▸ An *out-of-depth character*, such as a person pretending to be a vet having to treat a tortoise
- ▸ A *misunderstanding*, such as a prospective interviewee for a teaching job criticising the headmistress to another candidate, only to find on entering the interview that he has in fact been talking to the headmistress herself
- ▸ A short scene based on a *comic strip* story.

Tips

- ▸ Keep the scene short and to the point and use a *mixture of camera shots*.

- ▸ Create comic effects by combining straight pictures with an unexpected soundtrack, such as animal noises over pictures of school dinners.

- ▸ To mix sound with pictures, you need to connect a *sound source*, such as a cassette player, and a VCR with your videotape to a sound mixer. This should be connected to a master video recorder and a television monitor. You will also need headphones linked to the sound mixer (see diagram).

The sound-editing process

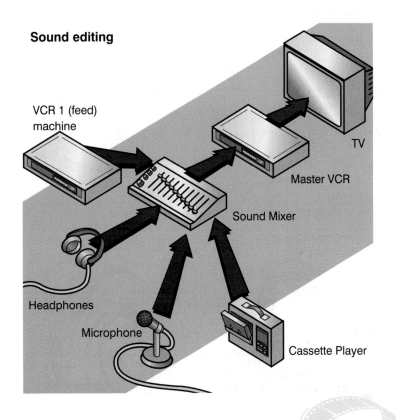

Sound editing

VCR 1 (feed) machine

TV

Master VCR

Sound Mixer

Headphones

Microphone

Cassette Player

Filming techniques

The establishing shot
Tells the audience where a scene takes place, e.g. the exterior of a block of New York apartments at the beginning of a scene from *Friends*.

The long shot
Shows the subject in the distance.

The medium shot
Focuses more closely on the subject than a long shot. Usually, a medium shot of a person shows the face and most of the body.

The close-up
The audience can see the face and shoulders of the character, but not the rest of the body.

Extreme close-up
The audience sees only part of the face of the subject. Can be used to reveal or to conceal:

- A close-up of a gun in someone's hand **reveals** imminent violence.
- A gloved hand on a door handle **conceals** the identity of a potential killer.

Filming techniques *(contd)*

High-angle shots
High-angle shots have the opposite effect: they make the person appear vulnerable.

Low-angle shots
If you film from a low angle it can have the effect of making the person appear more dominant.

Panning, zooming and tracking

Zooming
Zooming in makes things appear larger. Zooming out has the opposite effect. Zooming should be used sparingly and have a definite purpose: if you use zooming in and out too much it will irritate the audience.

Sometimes a slow zoom into a character's face can create tension.

Panning
Camera stays in one spot but moves horizontally in an arc.

Tracking
The camera moves, following the action.

Professionals use tracks laid like a miniature railway, along which the camera is moved. You can improvise by attaching the tripod to a base fitted with wheels.

Tracking shots can make a viewer feel involved in the action.

Panning hints

- Keep the movement smooth, using a tripod if you can.
- Hold the shot for a few seconds before and after the pan to help when you edit.
- Pan more slowly than you think is necessary.

- Try to finish on something interesting.
- Don't pan backwards and forwards – it unsettles the viewer.
- Use pans sparingly. They are useful for establishing a place or following some action.

The point of view shot

Abbreviated to **POV** in shooting scripts. Shows the audience what the character sees without revealing the character.

The cutaway

Shot used to help in the editing process, particularly in filmed interviews. Cutaways are brief shots of static items in the room which tell you something about the interviewee. These can be edited into the interview later to add interest or to cover gaps or mistakes.

Film a short suspense sequence.

The aim here is to film a 2-minute sequence from a thriller of your own devising and add a soundtrack with atmospheric music.

Here is a sample shooting script:

Shot 1	Two people (**A** and **B**) are tiptoeing along a corridor towards a distant door.
Shot 2	We see **A** keeping close to the wall and saying nervously, 'It's in there.'
Shot 3	**B**, crouching, says: 'I think I can hear it.'
Shot 4	We see the partly opened door. It creaks open a little more. **A** says: 'Be careful!'
Shot 5	**B** sidles through the doorway.
Shot 6	We see a POV shot from **B**'s perspective of a tall-backed chair. Strange breathing comes from it and there is something nasty on the arm of the chair.
Shot 7	We see a close-up of something nasty on the arm of the chair.
Shot 8	The camera moves in closer to the back of the chair. **A** cries: 'No, don't!' *There are gunshots.*
Shot 9	We see character **B** holding a smoking gun, there is a pause and then ...
Shot 10	We see a close-up of **B**'s face. He/she looks wide-eyed in terror and screams.... *Fade to black.* Throughout there is quiet, melancholy mouth-organ music – no tune, just sounds.

Write an evaluation of the film you have made.

What audience do you think it would appeal to? Would the film be unsuitable for certain age groups?

What planning and practice did you do and what did you learn from this? How could the film be improved?

For advice on how to write evaluations, see page 51.

Chapter 8

Newspapers *(1)*

> > *This chapter covers:*
- types of newspaper
- reporting styles
- classifying news stories
- newspaper circulation and readership
- content analysis
- newspaper opinion
- comparing the 'popular' and 'quality' press
- exam practice.

 **READING THE MEDIA**

Newspaper types

Tabloids and broadsheets

Originally, the word **tabloid** was applied to medicine in tablet form and meant 'compressed' or 'concentrated'. Tabloid-size newspapers were more concentrated than **broadsheets** and were introduced because people found them easier to read while travelling. The two terms **tabloid** and **broadsheet** have come to refer to the style and content of the two main types of newspaper.

- **Broadsheets** tend to be associated with more **upmarket readers** (people who are well-off and have good jobs).

- **Tabloids** are associated with a more **downmarket readership** (people who are less well-off and have lower-grade jobs).

Broadsheets are thought to contain more **serious** news, while tabloids are meant to be more **entertaining**. However, such simple comparisons can be misleading.

Broadsheet newspapers such as *The Guardian* have tabloid supplements and people from all walks of life read *The Sun*. Although *The Times* (a so-called 'quality' broadsheet) attracts 87% of its readers from the top social classes (ABC1), *The Sun* (popular tabloid) has roughly three times as many ABC1 readers than *The Times* because of its much larger readership.

Regional, local and free newspapers

In addition to the national daily newspapers, there are also **regional, local and free newspapers**, which can be either broadsheet or tabloid, though they mainly follow a tabloid format.

- **Regional** newspapers contain both regional and national news because they often compete for readership with the nationals. Local newspapers tend to be evening papers, concentrating on local stories from their own town or county.

- **Freesheets** are delivered to large numbers of people and contain huge amounts of advertising and small amounts of news. They tend to be produced weekly, though there are some morning papers in cities which are given out mainly to people travelling to work.

Analysing newspapers

Conduct research into newspaper types.

Visit a local newsagent and make a list of all the newspapers on display. Perhaps the newsagent can supply you with a list.

*Newspapers are printed in different sizes. Mark on your list which are **tabloid** and which are **broadsheet**. Underline any newspaper which is **local** or **regional**. Write FS next to any which are **free**.*

*Identify ways in which the newsagent **markets** (sells) newspapers.*

▸ *Look for the way they are displayed. Find out whether there is a delivery service, and ask why some papers are more prominently displayed than others (e.g. by being placed on the counter next to the till).*

▸ *Identify techniques used by the **newspapers** to increase sales.*

▸ *Look for price cuts, special offers, striking headlines and/or pictures, headlines on boards outside the shop and so on.*

*Skim-read a broadsheet and a tabloid newspaper and write down as many **similarities** and **differences** as you can.*

▸ *For example, both tabloid and broadsheet newspapers publish photographs, but the photographs in tabloids tend to take up more space on the page.*

Classify news stories from two newspapers.

Compare stories from two newspapers. Good pairs of newspapers to compare would be The Daily Mirror *and* The Daily Telegraph, *the* Daily Mail *and your local paper, or* The Guardian *and the* Daily Star.

Skim-read the stories and decide which of the categories listed in the table below best describes their content. Prepare a chart or copy the example below to show which categories of news are given most space.

Story category	Number of occurrences		
	Paper 1	*Paper 2*	*Paper 3*
Crime			
Unusual things happening to ordinary people			
Celebrities			
Money/wealth/poverty			
Medical			
Employment/industry			
Tragedies			
Lucky people/winners			
Politics			
Foreign news			
Sport			
Fashion			
Health			
New inventions or ideas			

Investigate the business side of newspapers.

Information about a newspaper's **circulation** and **readership** is of interest to **advertisers**.

- **Circulation** means the number of newspapers sold.
- **Readership** is the number of people who read the paper. This figure is usually larger than circulation because several people can read the same copy of a newspaper.

The charges for advertising space are related to a newspaper's circulation and readership. The bigger these are, the higher the charges.

Compile current newspaper readership figures. These can be found on the **National Readership Survey website** www.nrs.co.uk/reports/newspapers.htm

Study the information presented in the table opposite. Which paper has the biggest readership? On average, how many readers does it have per day? What proportion of the male population over 15 reads it?

| Daily newspaper | Average readership | | | | | |
| | Adults (15+) | | Men | | Women | |
	000s	%	000s	%	000s	%
The Sun	9,591	20.5	5,458	24.0	4,133	17.3
The Daily Mail	5,564	11.9	2,773	12.2	2,790	11.7
The Daily Telegraph	2,235	4.8	1,242	5.5	994	4.2
Daily Express	2,168	4.6	1,141	5.0	1,028	4.3
The Times	1,575	3.4	932	4.1	644	2.7
Daily Star	1,460	3.1	1,032	4.5	427	1.8
The Guardian	1,024	2.2	567	2.5	458	1.9
Financial Times	598	1.3	439	1.9	159	0.7
The Independent	571	1.2	333	1.5	238	1.0

Analyse the content of a newspaper.

Working in pairs, choose a newspaper to analyse and find out in detail what it contains. Start with the obvious things:

▶ How many pages are there?
▶ Are there any supplements or leaflets with the paper?
▶ What, briefly, is on each page? (For example, page 5 might consist of three national news stories, two photographs and a quarter-page advert.)

From this information, work out roughly how many pages are given to the categories listed below and present your findings to the rest of the class in the form of a table:

▶ News
▶ Listings (e.g. TV programmes, fixture lists)
▶ Advertising
▶ Photographs
▶ Opinion (editorials and columnists)
▶ Reader opinion (letters)
▶ Cartoons
▶ Gossip and showbiz trivia
▶ Advice (e.g. problem page)

▶ On-page activities (e.g. crosswords)
▶ Competitions
▶ 'How-to' articles (e.g. recipes, gardening tips)
▶ Business and finance
▶ Sport
▶ Fashion
▶ Health and fitness
▶ Motoring
▶ Holidays
▶ Other.

Investigate opinions and attitudes in newspapers.

Select a newspaper. Read the **editorials** and state briefly what **opinions** are expressed about different topics.

*Look at **columnists** and summarise their opinions.*

▸ *Columnists are journalists who express their opinions, e.g. Richard Littlejohn in* The Sun *or Lynda Lee-Potter in the* Daily Mail.

*Read a **letters** page in a daily newspaper and summarise the topics and opinions of the letters that have been selected.*

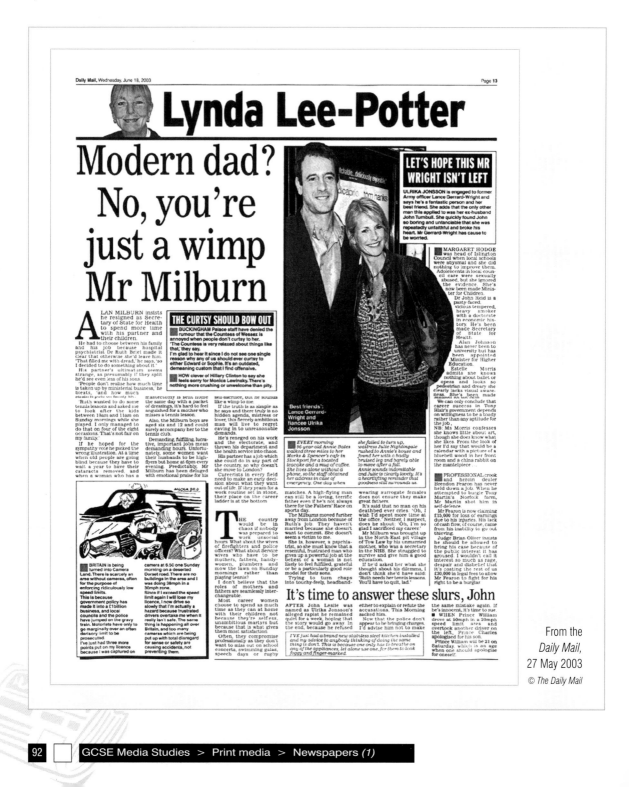

From the
Daily Mail,
27 May 2003
© The Daily Mail

Compare reporting styles in tabloids and broadsheets.

Look at the two contrasting newspaper extracts on pages 94–96. Both are based on the same story. One report is from the broadsheet newspaper The Guardian *and the other is from the popular tabloid* The Sun.

Use the questions and guidelines below to describe and analyse them.

*First of all, compare the **layout** of the two stories.*

▶ *What **conventions** do you spot (i.e. things which you would normally associate with newspapers, such as headlines and photographs with caption)?*

▶ *How is the story arranged on the page? How is the text shaped around the pictures? What is the proportion of pictures to text?*

▶ *Look at the **headlines**. Which paper uses more headlines? Compare the different sorts of type (fonts) used in the headlines.*

▶ *What highlighting devices are used by each paper (e.g. reverse print, capitals, large print, underlining, italics)?*

▶ *Which aspects of the story are emphasised by the headlines (e.g. punishment, the crime, the motives, the consequences)?*

*Look at the way each paper has used **photographs.***

▶ *The same pictures were available to both newspapers, but how many has each paper used? What differences are there in the way the pictures have been used?*

*Look at the **captions** under the pictures.*

▶ *How are they different? Describe the particular caption format which* The Sun *uses. How do* The Sun*'s captions emphasise the drama of the events?*

*From which **sources** did the journalists gather their information?*

▶ *Where have they been and whom have they interviewed?*

▶ *Which important interview does* The Sun *have which* The Guardian *does not have? How might* The Sun*'s reporter have achieved this?*

*Compare the **angles** taken by the journalists. An **angle** is a way of looking at events and focusing on a particular viewpoint.*

▶ *How does* The Sun *emphasise the religious element of the story?*

▶ *Compare* The Guardian*'s description of Phillips as a 'devout Christian' who told the police that the killing was 'God's way', with* The Sun*'s descriptions of him as 'The churchgoer from hell', 'God's vengeance dad', 'a God-fearing monster', 'Godman', etc.*

Which words in The Sun*'s report suggest madness or wildness?*

*How do you **respond** to the two styles of reporting?*

▶ *Which style do you prefer? Which are you most likely to take seriously?*

▶ *To what extent does the more dramatic tabloid style of* The Sun *turn the news into a form of entertainment?*

*In February 2000, a number of national daily newspapers
covered the trial at Birmingham Crown Court of Anthony
Phillips, a Methodist church steward from Wolverhampton
who was convicted of murdering his next-door neighbour
after discovering that she had been conducting an affair
with his sixteen-year-old son.*

*Here and on pages 95-96 are two contrasting accounts
of the trial hearings. The first* (below) *was recounted in*
The Guardian. *The second depiction of events* (opposite
and page 96) *was printed in* The Sun.

National News

Man gets life for axe murder of son's lover

Helen Carter

A devout Christian who hacked
his son's former lover to death
with an axe was jailed for life for
murder yesterday.

Anthony Phillips, a methodist
church steward from
Wolverhampton, beheaded his
next door neighbour, Lorraine
Howell, after discovering his
sixteen-year-old son had
fathered her daughter.

He called at Mrs Howell's
home last May and decapitated
her in front of her nine-year-old
son, James. Her six-month-old
baby was asleep in another
room.

Sentencing Phillips to life
imprisonment, Mr Justice
Latham said: 'As a result of that
obsession which you had over
the relationship between
Lorraine and your son, you not
only committed a cold and
calculated murder, as the jury
have quite properly found, but
you have destroyed the lives of
your family, and in particular
the family of Lorraine Howell.'

Birmingham Crown Court had
heard that Jamie Phillips began

an affair with Mrs Howell, 34, in
August 1997. They only had sex
on three occasions, but she
became pregnant early in 1998
and their baby daughter was
born in November.

[Jamie's] father felt
overriding hatred towards Mrs
Howell and was abusive to her
in the street. After his arrest he
told police that it was God's way
and he had been protecting
society.

The jury took fifty minutes
yesterday to reach a unanimous
verdict of murder.

Earlier, Tony Nayani, a
psychiatrist, told the jury that
he believed Phillips was
suffering from an abnormality of
mind when he killed his
neighbour.

Phillips, 43, said in police
interviews: 'It may be crude in
the way I have reached
retribution, but there was no
other way.'

He denied murder, but
admitted manslaughter on the
grounds of diminished
responsibility. He claimed that
Mrs Howell was a paedophile

rapist for sleeping with his son
when the boy was only 15.

Dr Nayani said that Phillips
had an intense concept of good
and evil and could see nothing
in between. Phillips believed
Mrs Howell had enticed his son
and should have been
prosecuted for it.

Seven weeks before the
murder, Phillips bought an axe
from a local store. His wife
Susan had told the court that
she believed Mrs Howell had
taken advantage of her innocent
son. 'My husband was quite
shocked and distressed,' she
said. 'He was a very highly moral
man. He could not believe our
son had let us down.'

She said he returned from
murdering Mrs Howell and said:
'She's dead.'

Outside the court, Mrs
Howell's mother, Isobel Weston,
said: 'We, her family, were
devastated by her death and we
are still in shock now. We can at
least be satisfied that justice
has been done.'

The Guardian,
25 February 2000

© The Guardian

The Sun's coverage of the story was divided into three parts. The main story, under the label 'SUN EXCLUSIVE', was this:

THE CHURCHGOER FROM HELL
Joy as 'God's vengeance' dad is jailed for life

A GOD-FEARING monster who beheaded a mum for bedding his fifteen-year-old son was caged for life yesterday.

Murdering Methodist Tony Phillips was led from the dock as his victim's ex husband screamed: 'Suffer, you bastard.'

Anguished Peter Howell, 43, said outside court: 'He should be strung up.

'*He was a hypocrite of the worst kind – the churchgoer from hell.*'

Pretty ex-wife Lorraine, 34, began the affair after Peter quit their Wolverhampton semi.

She later had a baby by Phillips's son Jamie.

Jamie, by then 16, tried to keep it from his bible-bashing dad – who was outraged when he found out.

Axe-wielding Phillips, 43 – who claimed temporary insanity – hacked off Lorraine's head in front of her sobbing nine-year-old boy James.

Haunted

The brute told cops it was 'the Lord's will.'

Jobless lorry driver Peter, who is now taking care of James, said: 'The boy is haunted by the image of his dead mother.

'*He has dreadful nightmares – I've seen him thrashing about in his sleep making stabbing movements with his arm.*

'*It breaks your heart. I hope Phillips rots in hell.*'

Silver-haired Phillips – an elder at nearby Brooklands methodist church – bought a £9 axe from B&Q to wreak his terrible revenge.

Frantic youngster James rushed to dial 999 as his mum was attacked – then dropped the receiver to try to help her.

The operator heard him cry out to the man who had often taken him to worship: 'Leave my mummy alone.' Dad Peter, who is now remarried, added: 'Lorraine didn't deserve to die like she did. She was a good mother.'

Workmates of factory maintenance man Phillips told how they used to call him 'Godman'.

One said: 'Other men had Page Three photos in their lockers. He had pictures of Jesus. He once had a sticker which read: "Thou shalt not kill."'

Methodist Minister Rev Alec Bailey, who visited Phillips on remand in prison, described him as 'devout'.

Lorraine was butchered feet from the Moses basket in which lay baby Lauren – her daughter by her young lover.

The tot, now 15 months old, is being cared for by her grandparents Isobel and Brian.

Isobel, 62, was at Birmingham Crown Court yesterday. Cheers erupted as a jury found Phillips guilty of murder. Judge Mr Justice Latham branded the killing 'cold and calculated'.

He told Phillips: 'You have destroyed the life of your family and particularly the family of Lorraine Howell'.

Isobel shouted as her daughter's killer was led away: 'Go, you bastard.'

Later she and her husband Brian, 62, said in a statement: 'Lorraine was a devoted mum and a well-liked person who always thought of her family first.'

Traumatised

Phillips' wife Sue, a Sunday school teacher, was not in court. Detective Sgt Mack Marpole said she and her son Jamie were also victims of the hideous crime.

He said: 'Mother and son have been traumatised and their lives have been ruined by it.'

Lorraine's ex-husband met Jamie for the first time during the three-day trial. He said: '*I have no problem with Jamie Phillips. He's suffering as well.*'

(contd on page 96)

Broadsheet and tabloid reporting

Of the other two stories making up The Sun's package, one, under the headline 'Lorraine's sex bid to hide the truth', is a background piece telling of Mrs Howell's relationship with Jamie and her ex-husband. The other report is reproduced here.

JURY TOOK JUST 45mins

THE jury took just 45 minutes to declare evil Tony Phillips sane and convict him of Lorraine's murder.

Phillips had pleaded guilty to manslaughter on the grounds of diminished responsibility. But he denied murder.

Defence psychiatrists claimed that as Phillips butchered Lorraine he heard voices and saw the face of the devil. He told detectives her death was a 'retribution' and that God told him to do it.

But the jurors threw out his claim that he acted on impulse.

Seething Phillips bought his B and Q axe – and made steps so he could climb over Lorraine's fence.

▸ *Does the heightened drama and excitement of the tabloid version encourage readers to respond in a more emotional way? If so, what emotions do you think the piece is intended to arouse?*

▸ *Note how from time to time in the tabloid version the text is italicised or printed in bold to imitate the way in which people change their tone of voice to make something sound more urgent or important. How does this affect your response to the article?*

Making media texts

See the activities at the end of Chapter 9.

Exam practice ▬▬▬▬▬

Select two contrasting newspapers such as a broadsheet and a tabloid (e.g. *The Independent* and *The Sun*). Read the front pages carefully for 30 minutes or so, making notes if you wish. Then answer these questions:

1 In what ways are the two front pages

   a different

   b similar?

2 Describe the effects of the main photographs. Explain how these are achieved through:

   a choice of words

   b images

   c layout.

3 What other features on the front pages might persuade a reader to read these papers?
4 With detailed reference to the pages, state the target audience for each paper and how you think these newspapers aim to attract those audiences.
5 Describe briefly three newspaper conventions, as featured on the front pages of one of the newspapers.
6 Describe briefly the layout of one of the front pages.
7 How have the photographs been used to attract an audience?
8 You are required to design the front page of a new local newspaper.

    a Suggest a title for the paper.
    b Suggest the kind of story you would like to feature on the front page and make up a headline for it.
    c Draw a layout for the front page to show where title, headlines and pictures would go.
    d Write notes to explain your layout and design.

Newspapers (2)

> > *This chapter covers:*

- news sources
- how news is selected
- how news is processed
- the influence of women journalists
- the portrayal of women in the press
- press freedom and people's right to privacy
- the history of *The Sun*
- newspaper finance
- designing a school/college newspaper
- writing stories and editorials from press releases and interviews.

READING THE MEDIA

Where does news come from?

About two-thirds of all news stories come from press releases or press conferences.

- **Press releases** are written by public relations (PR) professionals in order to provide the news media with ready-made stories. An example of a press release is shown on page 111.

Dramatic events like the attack on the World Trade Center on September 11 2001 have immediate impact around the globe

▪ A **press conference** is a meeting at which journalists are briefed about a topic or news story, and can put questions directly to the people involved. For example, when a football club signs a new player, it will call a press conference to introduce the player to the media, arrange for photographs and television pictures to be taken and schedule interviews.

Many organisations seek publicity, including:

▪ political parties
▪ government departments
▪ local authorities
▪ trade unions
▪ employers' organisations
▪ pressure groups (e.g. the Child Poverty Action Group)
▪ consumer groups (e.g. the National Consumer Council)
▪ environmental movements (e.g. Greenpeace).

Protests such as this demonstration against the war in Iraq held in London in March 2003 attract worldwide media coverage

Many **commercial organisations** also want to draw their successes to the public's attention, while some **individuals** such as celebrities, authors, performers and researchers use the news media to publicise their work.

Events or happenings attract attention. These range from the devastation of terrorist attacks to the staging of demonstrations and peace protests.

Other sources of news include:

- parliament
- **diary events** which are planned and to which the media are invited (e.g. political party conferences)
- the **emergency services** – fire brigade, police and ambulance
- the **law courts**
- **members of the public** who contact the news organisation with complaints or tip-offs.

News organisations can also start their own **investigations**.

Working in pairs, look at the stories opposite and match them to the possible sources listed above.

Note: *There will sometimes be more than one possible source.*

Look at all the stories in today's newspaper and work out the source of as many items as possible.

'Steve McFadden's manager said: "Angie's a lovely girl and they're both thrilled."'

'England soccer star Paul Gascoigne was given a three-month suspended jail sentence ...'

'An angry motorist is blamed for a road rage attack – on a speed camera. Police won't say if ...'

'Having a good moan about your problems lessens depression and cuts the risk of a heart attack, according to German researchers.'

'The prototype computer was unveiled by IBM in Hanover, Germany...'

'Dunblane parents yesterday launched a shock ad with 007 legend Sean Connery in a bid to get all handguns banned. Campaigners hope ...'

'Downing Street suddenly decided last night not to seek the return of British prisoners from Camp X-Ray after an ultimatum from the Americans.'

'Ecstasy consumption in Britain could be four times higher than official figures, according to a confidential police report.'

'A doctor was accused yesterday of making only a cursory examination of a girl who died just hours later from meningitis.'

'Ferdinand said that Leeds United had developed him as a player, but he was happy now to have signed for Manchester United.'

How is news selected?

It is the job of the **news editor** to **select** which items or stories to print. News editors also have to **prioritise** the stories – that is, to give more prominence to some than to others.

In order to do this, they need to know the kinds of stories their **readers** like and the kind of newspaper they want to produce.

Rupert Murdoch, who owns media organisations throughout the world and is proprietor of News International, which publishes *The Sun* and *The Times* among others, had this to say about what he thought **readers wanted**:

> 'I think we speak for common sense and we understand working-class values. It's a mixture of morality and hedonism … we want them to have a good time yet have strong values.'

Larry Lamb, a former editor of *The Sun*, said that his readers were not interested in politics, philosophy and economics, but wanted to read about 'things like food and money, sex and crime, football and television'.

Here are some of the reasons why a particular story may be chosen to be covered in the press:

- It is significant from a **human interest** point of view (e.g. 'mother and child die in blaze')
- It is **dramatic** and exciting (e.g. yachtswoman in danger as she tries to complete her round-the-world voyage)
- The **personalities** involved are well known (e.g. Madonna's wedding)
- It is **odd** or rarely happens (e.g. 100-year-old woman does bungee jump)
- It is an example of **progress** (e.g. advances in medicine)
- It has **visual appeal** – and there is a **good picture** available to illustrate it
- There is a possible or real **scandal** (e.g. President Clinton and Monica Lewinsky)
- It is about **crime**
- It is significant **socially** (e.g. race riots in Bradford and Oldham)
- It is significant **economically** (e.g. the Chancellor's Budget, news of major job losses)
- It is significant **politically** (e.g. Prime Minister orders cabinet re-shuffle, reform of the National Health Service).

Working in pairs or small groups, study the news stories opposite and match them to the categories above.

Note: A story may fit more than one category.

'The huddled, frozen bodies of 19 asylum seekers, a group which included six women and nine children, were discovered yesterday in a remote mountain region of south-eastern Turkey.'

'An 18-month-old boy underwent reconstructive facial surgery this week after he was mauled by his family's pet dog.'

'Claude Williams, 41, a former member of the group Massive Attack, has been jailed for 18 months for beating up a man in a bail hostel.'

'Euro MPs have voted against changes to the car market which could have cut the price of new cars by £2000.'

'Guilty verdicts on pig farmer.'

'Another exam board apologises after setting questions without answers.'

'25 million ecstasy tablets were seized worldwide last year.'

'WILDFLOWERS STUDY GIVES CLEAR EVIDENCE OF GLOBAL WARMING.'

'Planes combed the jungles of Colombia near the Patia river yesterday after a radio distress call renewed hope that two Canadians and a French man were alive six weeks after their helicopter disappeared.'

'Britain is opposing proposals to post EU border guards at ports and airports to combat illegal immigration.'

Collect a week's newspapers. From them, find examples of news stories of each of the story types listed on the right. Cut out an example of each category and make a display under the heading 'News Values'.

From your investigation, which of the categories had the most examples? Make a note of this on your display and suggest a reason for this.

Press images of women

A survey by a group called Women in Journalism analysed the way women are portrayed in newspapers. It found that photographs of women are more likely to be of celebrities and members of the public than politicians, sportswomen or professionals.

The group gave these examples of what typically happens:

- In a story about a south London group of six men and six women involved in an 'air rage' incident, the pictures used showed only young, blonde women.
- In an unexciting story about the launch of the website *Totalise*, the staged publicity shot included the (male) chief executive on a surfboard surrounded by Baywatch-type females. The picture used was cropped (cut back) to show just the women.
- A business story in *The Times* about the leisure firm LA Fitness carried a picture of three male executives standing behind an apparently naked blonde woman in a Jacuzzi soaping a raised leg.

Of the 12,000 pictures analysed by the group, women were featured in only **42%** of pictures of celebrities and members of the public, **25%** of pictures of professionals and **2%** of pictures of sportspeople.

Rebekah Wade, chairwoman of Women in Journalism and now editor of *The Sun*, said, 'Our research shows that women are significantly under-represented in newspapers, even though they make up almost half the readers.'

Women in Journalism also contrasted the press portrayal of two MPs who left the Conservative party to join another party. The man, Alan Howarth, was portrayed as wrestling with an agonising moral dilemma. The woman, Emma Nicholson, was portrayed as a flighty woman who probably fancied Paddy Ashdown, leader of the party she joined.

Story types

- human interest
- action/drama
- well-known personality
- odd, rare or unusual event
- scientific advance or breakthrough
- visual/picture-led story
- crime
- social
- economic
- political

This picture was used in a press report about an 'air rage' incident. Although six men and six women were involved, the photograph showed only participants who were young, female and blonde

Newspaper history: *The Sun*

1911 Starts life as *The Daily Herald,* a newssheet for London print unions.

1961 Declining circulation of the *Herald* leads to it being sold to the *Daily Mirror* group.

1964 The paper is renamed and launched as *The Sun*. Aimed at the 'middle-class couple, aged 28 with two children, and living in Reading' who want an intelligent and mature newspaper, it fails to find its market and does not prosper.

1969 The paper is bought by Rupert Murdoch for £600,000. It concentrates on 'sex, sport and sensation', competing directly for readers with parent paper the *Mirror*. By its third day, *Sun* circulation has risen to 1,650,000.

1970 First topless 'Page 3' picture.

1970 Firmly supports Labour at the election...

1974 ... then switches to the Tories.

1981 Kelvin MacKenzie appointed editor. MacKenzie soon demonstrates flair for appealing to the tastes, opinions and prejudices of the English working class.

1987 An Elton John story lands *The Sun* in trouble with the law. It has to pay £1 million in libel costs to the pop musician.

1989 Under the headline 'The Truth', runs front-page story about the Hillsborough disaster in which 95 Liverpool football fans were crushed to death. As a result of critical comments in the article about the behaviour of some Liverpool fans, sales of the paper in the Liverpool area plummet and the editor is forced to apologise.

1990 When Thatcher is ousted, the paper criticises the Tory party rather than Thatcher in particular. It also brands the England football team 'World Cup Wallies' – but the team does well and reaches the semi-final. The paper changes tack and praises 'our heroes'. But it seems to have lost touch with its readers.

1992 Claims to have been responsible for defeating Neil Kinnock and Labour at the election: 'IT'S THE SUN WOT WON IT'.

1994 MacKenzie replaced as editor. The paper becomes less critical of government and less adventurous.

1997 'THE SUN BACKS BLAIR – Give change a chance'.

Another contrast was shown between the coverage of two climbers killed in mountaineering accidents. Alison Hargreaves, a mother, was criticised for doing something as dangerous as climbing when she should have been looking after her children. The male victim, Geoff Tier, a father, never had his right to climb questioned, and his fatherhood was never made an issue.

Eve Pollard of Women In Journalism recalls working on a tabloid newspaper where, as soon as a woman featured in a story, the sub-editors would ask: 'What colour is her hair?' If she was a blonde, she immediately became a 'bubbly blonde'; if brunette, she was described as a 'sultry brunette'; and if red, she was a 'fiery redhead'.

A survey commissioned by Women in Journalism in 1996 found:

- 88% of women surveyed thought that newspapers were prejudiced against their gender
- 50% of those who named one paper as the worst offender picked *The Sun* (although not all of these women had read this paper)
- 20% of female *Sun* readers thought this paper biased against women
- 75% of women surveyed could not name a single paper which was 'on their side'
- of those who could name a paper slanted towards women, 23% nominated the *Daily Mail*. No other paper came close.

READING THE MEDIA — Representation of women in the press

Look at the way men and women are portrayed in The Sun, *the* Daily Mirror *and the* Star *in the course of a week and work out the proportion of male to female pictures. What proportion of photographs attempts to present men or women in a decorative or glamorous light?*

Find examples of the use of phrases such as:

- *'mum of two'*
- *'pretty young waitress'*
- *'curvy Roberta'*
- *'former Guards and SAS officer'*
- *'stunning Melanie and her soldier hubby'*
- *'brave Lawrence'*
- *'jubilant Warriors coach'.*

What gender differences do you notice?

In parts of the paper which are targeted at women, what topics are covered? What conclusions do you draw from the research done by Women in Journalism and your own findings?

Present your conclusions as a report to the rest of your group. Illustrate your report with cuttings, charts and/or graphs.

Press freedom and privacy

Read the case study below, then discuss these questions:

▸ *Should there be a difference between famous people and 'ordinary' people as far as publicity is concerned?*

▸ *Should members of the public have a right to know anything they might find of interest? Or should some things remain private?*

▸ *How can journalists find out things which people want to keep secret?*

▸ *Are there any methods of journalistic investigation that should be banned?*

Case Study
Privacy and censorship

MP George Galloway describes what happened when journalists started investigating his private life.

Everyone from my elderly grandmother ... to our neighbours was besieged by large numbers of journalists.

Outside my home for 48 hours there were upwards of 20 journalists and photographers encamped. They even stayed overnight with little Primus stoves and camp beds, though they made it impossible for people in the house to sleep by ringing the doorbell and knocking on the window throughout the night.

The next day my five-year-old daughter was chased down the path into her primary school. Later a photographer told the caretaker that he was her uncle come to take her home for her protection.

Someone stole my telephone card index, and every single woman in it, from 15 to 90, was systematically phoned and asked, not if they *had,* but would they like to talk about their affair with me – when none of them had ever had an affair with me.

Many of them had their houses staked out. A woman in Glasgow was offered £1,000 by *The Sun* to tell of her affair with me when she had never had an affair with me.

Press intrusion

The Press Complaints Commission states that intrusions into a person's private life are *not* acceptable unless in the **public interest**.

The public interest includes:

- detecting or exposing crime
- detecting or exposing serious anti-social behaviour
- protecting public health and safety
- preventing the public being misled by a statement or action of the individual.

It also prohibits the photographing of children under the age of 16 without the consent of the parent or another responsible adult.

Press freedom

The National Union of Journalists code of conduct states:

'A journalist shall defend the principle of freedom of the press in relation to the collection of information. He or she shall strive to eliminate news suppression and censorship.'

and:

'A journalist shall obtain information, photographs and illustrations only by straightforward means. The use of other means can only be justified by overriding considerations of the public interest.'

Newspaper finance

Newspapers that are paid for earn revenue partly from their **sale price** and partly from **advertising**.

Advertising revenue is linked with circulation and readership *(see above)*. The more readers a newspaper has, the more it can charge for advertising space.

A **free newspaper** can claim a large circulation because the papers can be delivered to every household in a district. However, a paper delivered is not necessarily a paper read – and advertisers are more interested in numbers of readers than in numbers of deliveries.

A newspaper that is paid for can increase its circulation by selling large numbers of cut-price papers to organisations like hotels and fast-food outlets. These are called **bulk sales**. The papers are given free to customers, but again they may not be read.

Readership profiles

There are certain groups of people which are more attractive to advertisers than others. The 25–34 age group contains big spenders, especially on leisure pursuits and fashion. 'Main female shoppers' is another group which some advertisers are particularly eager to target. Consequently, *The Sun* emphasises in its media pack that it has over 4 million 'female main shoppers' and that 36% of its readers live in 'households with children aged 0–15'.

Certain socio-economic groups are particularly attractive to advertisers. These are:

- **ABs** (about 15% of the workforce): people who have professional or managerial jobs
- **C1s** (about 28% of working population): mainly people in skilled non-manual jobs.

The following groups are less attractive to advertisers:

- **C2s** (31%): people in skilled manual jobs
- **DEs** (25%): semi-skilled or unskilled manual workers, state pensioners and the unemployed.

This is how *The Sunday Times* 'sells' its magazine sections to potential advertisers:

> '*Culture* is read by 2.4 million readers, many of whom fall into the younger 25–44 age group. In fact, the magazine's younger and up-market contingent is growing. *Culture's* ABC1 25–44 readership has risen by 8%.'

Its *Style* magazine, it says, is:

> 'perfectly pitched at the lively, modern, stylish and health-conscious audience that make up *Sunday Times* readers'.

Current charges for advertising space can be found in BRAD (British Rate and Data), which is available in most libraries. In 2000, *The Sun* charged about £50,000 for a full-page colour advertisement.

Design and plan a school/college newspaper.

*When you are involved in producing a school newspaper, you should have a list of **aims**. Look through the list of suggestions below and then make up your own list of aims.*

▸ *Have a balance of news, opinions, advice and entertainment.*
▸ *Write in a style and tone that suits the target audience.*
▸ *Be topical and local.*
▸ *Conduct some original research.*
▸ *Present different points of view.*
▸ *Have a variety of features, e.g. quizzes, cartoons, crosswords and letters.*
▸ *Have reports on school/college sports.*
▸ *Have good quality, original photographs and graphics.*
▸ *Write captions for all pictures.*
▸ *Have a clear, easy-to-read layout.*
▸ *Have eye-catching headlines.*
▸ *Check that spelling and punctuation are accurate.*

*State who your **target audience** comprises in terms of age, gender, location and interests.*

▸ *Do some research into the interests of your target audience by interviewing people or asking them to fill in questionnaires. You could give them a list of possible topics and ask them to say how interested they would be in reading about them.*

*Produce a **four-page mock-up** of a section of your paper. You need a basic grid divided into columns. The design features you can use are boxes, colour tints, bullet points, different fonts and rules.*

▸ *Draw a rough plan for each page, showing where pictures and text would go. Include headlines/titles.*

A sample mock-up and a list of possible subjects for articles are shown on page 102.

*Make a list of the kinds of **advertising** you could attract for your target audience.*

*Write an **evaluation** of your pre-production mock-up, describing the research you did into your target audience's interests, the problems you came across and how you tried to solve them.*

▸ *What aspects of your design worked well and what didn't? Give reasons for your answer.*
▸ *Check your list of aims and state how far you achieved them.*

For advice about writing evaluations, see page 51.

Here are some ideas for articles you could include:

- Local entertainments listings
- Reviews/previews of records, films, gigs, videos, games, TV programmes, etc.
- Interviews with local bands
- 'Be a sex symbol this summer – the dos and don'ts of holiday romances'
- Report of a girl's date with a male model (a competition prize)
- Reports on progress of college/school sports teams
- Real-life stories of success and failure
- Problem pages (for both sexes)
- Holiday guides
- Fashions
- 'How-to' articles, e.g. organise a party, use the Internet
- Photo-stories
- A guide to local fitness gyms – do they give value for money?
- Shopping guides
- Competitions
- True confessions
- Back chat.

MAKING THE MEDIA

Writing feature articles for a newspaper

Write a story based on a press release.

As entertainments writer for your school/college newspaper, you have just received the press release below:

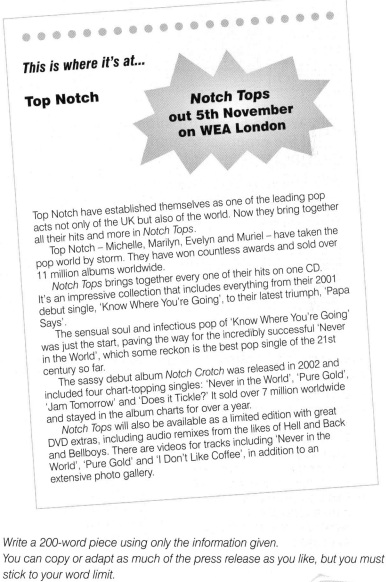

This is where it's at...

Top Notch

Notch Tops out 5th November on WEA London

Top Notch have established themselves as one of the leading pop acts not only of the UK but also of the world. Now they bring together all their hits and more in *Notch Tops*.

Top Notch – Michelle, Marilyn, Evelyn and Muriel – have taken the pop world by storm. They have won countless awards and sold over 11 million albums worldwide.

Notch Tops brings together every one of their hits on one CD. It's an impressive collection that includes everything from their 2001 debut single, 'Know Where You're Going', to their latest triumph, 'Papa Says'.

The sensual soul and infectious pop of 'Know Where You're Going' was just the start, paving the way for the incredibly successful 'Never in the World', which some reckon is the best pop single of the 21st century so far.

The sassy debut album *Notch Crotch* was released in 2002 and included four chart-topping singles: 'Never in the World', 'Pure Gold', 'Jam Tomorrow' and 'Does it Tickle?' It sold over 7 million worldwide and stayed in the album charts for over a year.

Notch Tops will also be available as a limited edition with great DVD extras, including audio remixes from the likes of Hell and Back and Bellboys. There are videos for tracks including 'Never in the World', 'Pure Gold' and 'I Don't Like Coffee', in addition to an extensive photo gallery.

Write a 200-word piece using only the information given.
You can copy or adapt as much of the press release as you like, but you must stick to your word limit.
Devise a simple competition to go with your article and give details of the prizes.

Write a story based on some research findings.

Read the survey of teenage lifestyles presented opposite. Use some or all of the information to produce an article for your newspaper on the subject of teenage lifestyles. The article should be between 300 and 500 words.

▸ *Make up headlines. Use the two graphs and add your own photographs, if possible.*
▸ *The layout should be in columns, newspaper-style.*
▸ *You can produce a compilation of small stories or write one long story.*
▸ *Include a cartoon if you like.*

MAKING THE MEDIA

Report on a controversy

Write a 300-word editorial (opinion piece) for your paper about the proposal to start an opencast mine at Warden Hill.

Use the information provided in the map below, the press releases on page 114 and the transcript of an interview with a local resident on page 115. Try to give both sides of the argument.

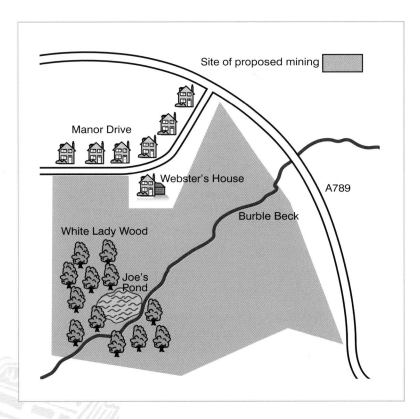

Map showing site of proposed open-cast mine at Warden Hill

Teenage lifestyles: survey findings

Sample: 18,000

Age range: 11–16

- 2% of boys and 1% of girls claim they drink alcohol every day of the week.
- 30% of 16-year-old boys bought alcohol in pubs, 19% used the off-licence, and 7% bought from supermarkets.
- Over 50% of 16-year-olds had been to a pub at least once in the last fortnight, mostly with their parents.
- Alcohol consumption among 16-year-olds ranged from half a pint of beer or one glass of wine per week to more than 10 pints of beer or 20 glasses of wine per week (7.4% of boys).
- 7% of 16-year-olds (boys and girls) did not want to give up smoking.
- Of regular smokers, 6% of boys and 4% of girls smoked more than 60 cigarettes per week.
- 20% of girls aged 15–16 skip breakfast.
- 11% of 16-year-old girls skip lunch.
- The popularity of school lunches declines as children grow older, almost halving between 11 and 16.
- 50% of 11-year-olds eat more than one packet of crisps per day.
- 20% of boys aged 11 and 10% of girls of the same age spend more than five hours each night watching television.

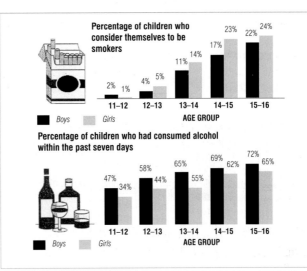

Research by Middle Britain University © The Guardian

- Among 16-year-olds, 60% of boys and 55% of girls said they had done no homework the previous night.
- Of the others, many spent up to two hours per night on homework, with girls working longer than boys.
- 50% of boys and 38% of girls aged 11 did not read books for pleasure. By 16 the figures were 68% (boys) and 54% (girls).
- 25% of all ages read a local newspaper regularly.
- 50% of all ages say they read a 'popular' newspaper.
- 33% of 11-year-olds claim to have a steady boyfriend or girlfriend.
- The proportion increases for girls by age 16 but remains about the same for boys.
- 50% of teenage relationships last only a few months.

When newspapers reported on these facts, these were some of the headlines used:

'Our mis-spent youth'

'Teen tipplers'

'Meal skippers'

'Books lose to box'

'Pupils take pub and homework in moderation'

'Kids with money to burn'

'Once-a-day drinkers'

'Fags: up to 60 a week'

Open-cast mining at Warden Hill: for and against

Press release

INDEPENDENT MINING LTD.

The company plans to excavate a site at Warden Hill and recover about 1 million tonnes of good quality coal.

The coal will be used in a nearby power station to provide electricity for the national grid, thereby helping to keep energy costs down for both industry and the domestic consumer.

This operation will provide work for about 50 people, most of whom will be recruited locally for three and a half years. This will help the local economy.

The site will be landscaped once the coal has been extracted. It will be transformed from its present dereliction into an attractive local amenity with woodland, ponds and recreation areas.

Disruption to the local community will be minimised. The number of lorries taking coal along Manor Road and on to the A789 will be restricted to ten per day.

95% of the dust from the site will fall within 500 metres of the site.

The company will consider paying compensation to any local business affected by the scheme.

The mine will also help the local economy because of the rates it will be paying to the council.

Press release

Greengrass

The proposed opencast mining at Warden Hill will be a complete disaster for the local environment. The area has precious wildlife which will be destroyed. Joe's Pond is a breeding ground for a rare species of frog. There are only five colonies of the Feral frog left in Britain.

The area of White Lady Wood is important too, as there are remnants of an ancient forest. The company can say it will landscape the site after it has taken the coal but you can't replace ancient woodland like this. Once it's gone, it's gone.

The area also provides recreation for local people. There is a pleasant path by Burble Beck, which is frequently used by people taking exercise, both cyclists and walkers.

A survey of local residents has shown that 90% oppose this destructive plan.

Interview with
Jim Webster

Jim Webster is leader of the protest group opposed to open-cast mining at Warden Hill

Reporter: You're the leader of the protest against the opencast mining scheme, Jim. Why's that?

JW: We think that this scheme, if God forbid it goes ahead, will make life intolerable for the people of the area. There is going to be so much dirt and noise it'll just be hell. At the moment it's a lovely area. It's countryside, a place to feel free in, to relax and enjoy and it's going to be turned into a noisy, polluted hell-hole. And people have paid a lot of money for their houses in Manor Drive and the value will just plummet overnight. It's not on.

Reporter: How are you involved personally? Apparently you have a business which will be affected?

JW: Very much so. I run a small guest house which will be right next to the proposed site. I mean, it'll just ruin me. At the moment, people come here for a peaceful out-of-town location with nice views, but who's going to want to stay next to an industrial eyesore?

Reporter: But hasn't the mining company promised to compensate you for loss of business?

JW: What they are offering is a joke. But anyway, it's not just about money, it's about our lives being changed. We don't want this. We actually like running a guest house. We like looking after people. Which is more than I can say for these industrial vandals.

Open-cast mining such as this will have serious long-term effects on the environment of Warden Hill, say protesters

Taking and using photographs: some guidelines

- Give your page variety by including different shapes and sizes of picture.
- Make sure every picture has a caption.
- Occasionally, make use of white space around illustrations. They do not have to be surrounded by text.

- Hold the camera still.
- Use your own body or the objects around you to support or steady the camera.

- Use a good picture as a main point of interest on a page. Note that the shape of a picture can be changed by cropping, enlarging, and allowing the picture to 'spill' out of its box.

Taking and using photographs (contd)

- Get close to people you are photographing. Most ordinary snapshots are taken from too far away.
- You don't have to position people so that they are looking straight at the camera. More interesting shots can be of people looking away from the camera in either a three-quarter view or in profile.

- Try to have the subject doing something or catch them when they are not aware of being photographed. This will produce more natural pictures.

- Diagonals can make a picture more interesting by giving it depth.

MAKING THE MEDIA

Produce a double-page spread for a newspaper

Use the articles you have written, and/or others you have devised yourself, to produce a double-page spread for a newspaper.

*Describe your **target audience** in terms of age, gender, location and interests.*
Design your pages as in the pre-production exercise above.
*Write an **evaluation** of your feature pages.*
*Describe any **research** you carried out into your audience interests. What design and production problems did you have and how well did you solve them? What reaction did you get from people who read your pages?*

For advice about writing evaluations, see page 51.

Magazines

>> *This chapter covers:*

- types of magazines and their audiences
- editorials and contents pages
- magazine ownership
- what target markets are
- an analysis of *Smash Hits* – editorial, images, texts, adverts
- producing a magazine cover
- exam practice – analyse and produce a magazine cover.

READING THE MEDIA

Types of magazine

There are many different types of magazine. They are usually aimed at small, specialised audiences rather than large, general audiences. Often, the title will indicate the type of magazine.

The first set of activities in this chapter will help you to become aware of the vast range of magazines available and the ways in which they concentrate on particular areas of interest. We then move on to take a detailed look at the audience and format of the teen magazine *Smash Hits*.

Front cover of a recent issue of *Heat* magazine

In pairs, look at the list of titles below and decide whether each indicates clearly its contents.

- *Campaign*
- *Farmers Weekly*
- *Art Monthly*
- *Black Media Journal*
- *Asian Times*
- *Empire*
- *PC Format*
- *Woman and Home*
- *Dancing Times*
- *House Beautiful*
- *Heat*
- *Match*
- *Amateur Gardening*
- *Horse and Hounds*
- *Loaded*
- *Mojo*
- *Climber*
- *Red*
- *CD:UK*

'If the title does not make the type of magazine clear, the main visual image usually succeeds.' Do some basic research to find out if this statement is true.

Make a collection of images from magazine covers without the headings and see if your friends can work out what type of magazine they are from.
Make a note of the reasons they give for their answers.

Make a collection of popular magazines (especially teenage magazines) which focus on celebrities.

Find examples of:

- *celebrities being portrayed as glamorous, sexy, powerful or rich*
- *celebrities being portrayed as ordinary or vulnerable.*

Make a display of images which show celebrities as both special and ordinary.
Make a display to show how males and females are portrayed differently. For instance, men are more likely to be photographed being mean and mysterious, whereas females are more likely to be shown in groups and being more tactile.

Editorials and contents pages

A magazine's **editorial** is usually printed near the front. It is written by the editor and its content and style will tell you what sort of magazine it is and what it thinks of its readers.

Here's an editorial from *Top of the Pops Magazine*:

Grrrr! Pop's gone kerrr-azy this month, so grab your geetar and get ready to rock. Here at *TOTP* Towers we've been perfecting our meanest snarls and leaping around the office like complete loons. In search of some handy hints, we paid a visit to Fred Durst, on p. 28. He took us on a tour of his Beverly Hills pad, and even let us have a shufty in his toy box!

Bottoms were at large when pop giants Destiny's Child nipped in for a chat. They may be the hottest babes on the block, but even they complain about the size of their butts!

One hot babe we never get enough of is cheeky chappie Noel from Hear'Say. Yep, this is the moment you've all been waiting for – his first ever solo cover! We get intimate with the most eligible bachelor in the business and find out what he looks for in a dream date.

Still not satisfied? Why not hang with Usher, p. 54, or watch Atomic Kitten squirm in their seats as they face the toughest interview in pop. Phew! And as the new resident scribblers at *TOTP* you'll be hearing a lot more from us in the future. Rock on!

Notice how the writers are trying to be:

- ▨ chatty (e.g. 'grab your geetar' and 'hang with')
- ▨ 'dangerous' (e.g. 'leaping like loons')
- ▨ exciting (see the number of exclamation marks they use!!)
- ▨ sexually aware without being coarse or crude.

Find two current editorials from different magazines. Describe what each one tells you about the magazine's content and its attitude to its readers.

Look carefully at the contents page of a magazine or look at the examples opposite.

Make a note of keywords or dominant ideas.

▸   *On the contents page of an issue of* Smash Hits, *for instance, there seems to be an excitement about* **revealing secrets***, giving inside information:*

–   *'Behind the scenes on their new video'*
–   *'Find out the truth behind all those pesky rumours'*
–   *'All the goss from the garage groover'*
–   *'Faithless reveal their love for boy bands'.*

Then there is the hint of **sex and excitement***:*

–   *'Their summer holiday frolics busted'*
–   *'in a showgirl romp'*
–   *'on his wild nights out'*
–   *'Lisa, Faye and Claire get fruity'*
–   *'rock and rudery'.*

'A law unto himself – why no-one but Clint Eastwood makes his day.'

'Bravehearts – mutual admiration society – our heroes name their heroes.'

'Courage under fire – reluctant Gulf War hero finds a captive audience.'

'Son of a Gunner – defender of the Arsenal faith Tony Adams talks the talk with Tom Watt.'

'The right man, the right stuff – Chris Hulme meets veteran test pilot Chuck Yeager, the first man to break the sound barrier.'

'Mack Bastable gives chicks the chat.'

'Ace of Spades on how to cheat at cards.'

'Ben Driver beats off impotence.'

'Stage your own Tour de France.'

'NYC as easy as ABC – the Big Apple's ten best hotels.'

'Cole Morton relives Teddy Sheringham's first kick.'

'Vision on. Treat your sofa like a friend.'

'The Kittens reveal their new band member. Or maybe we're lying.'

'The best rowing machines.'

'What's spookier? The alien or Howie's blouson?'

'Ring to win! If you're a lucky cookie, free stuff could be yours.'

'Let Tina entertain you with her top party tales ... or perhaps Rob's more your type of party pal? The choice is yours.'

'"Come back and see my etchings," H said to us. "Ooh young maaan!" we replied. But we went anyway.'

'Our Jonathan gets a bit of sun and sand in the desert with Bellefire!'

'Dec calls Jonathan Wilkes. Is yer flatmate in?'

'Pop Eye. No celeb can escape us!'

'It's boob and bus traumas for Westlife.'

Read the text of some magazine stories and try to work out where the stories have come from.

*Are readers being offered recycled press releases or the magazine writers' own thoughts? Are the articles speculations, gossip or facts? In other words, **who** is telling the stories and **with what purpose**?*

Magazine ownership

The teenage magazines listed in *The Writer's Handbook 2001* are:

* *BIG!*
* *Bliss*
* *J17*
* *Looks*
* *Mizz*
* *19*
* *Smash Hits*
* *Sugar*
* *Top of the Pops Magazine.*

All these teenage magazines are owned by the company EMAP. On its website, EMAP has a slightly different way of classifying magazines. It lists 'young women's and teens' magazines together *(see table below)*.

EMAP Magazines Circulation Figures

Title	Jan–Jul 2001	Jul–Dec 2000	Jan–Jul 2000	% Change Pd on Pd*	% Change Yr on Yr
Bliss	255,251	300,191	287,897	−15	−11.3
Celebrity Looks	130,088	132,032	133,150	n/a	−2.3
J-17	197,611	200,330	200,030	−1.4	−1.2
More!	300,281	305,344	300,234	−1.7	0
Smash Hits	198,621	221,622	250,388	−10.4	−20.7
19	117,021	133,890	148,244	−12.6	−21.1
B Magazine	200,836	216,620	209,820	−7.3	−4.3
Jump	n/a	n/a	n/a	n/a	n/a
Live & Kicking	94,504	116,255	140,168	−18.7	−32.6
Mizz	154,779	163,672	162,195	−5.4	−4.6
Shout	119,052	123,360	116,629	−3.5	2.1
Sugar	368,559	422,179	415,973	−12.7	−11.4
Top of the Pops	281,417	305,122	389,245	−7.8	−27.7
TV Hits	175,518	201,855	204,805	−13	−14.3
Star	130,493	n/a	n/a	n/a	n/a

* = Period on period. The change between the period Jul–Dec 2000 to Jan–Jul 2001

Study the table of circulation figures on page 122 and answer the questions below.

How many copies of Bliss, *the monthly magazine for teenage girls, were sold on average per month between January and June 2001?*

How many copies of Bliss *were sold on average per month between July and December 2000?*

What was the percentage change between these two figures?

Which magazine recorded the only year-on-year increase?

Which magazine had the biggest fall in year-on-year sales?

▶ *You can find up-to-date circulation figures on:*
   www.emapadvertising.com/magazines/abc/abc.asp

Magazine target audiences

EMAP classifies its magazines under these topics:

- boys
- entertainment
- girls
- glossy
- golf
- health
- home interest
- Internet
- men's
- motoring
- music.

You can tell that the magazines are aimed at specialist audiences by these EMAP categories, and by the way the company describes them to its advertisers:

Bliss

With its unique positioning as 'the mag that makes you famous', *Bliss* is the second biggest selling teen title. Under the editorship of Liz Nice, *Bliss* leads the market in editorial innovation and exciting new ideas such as the Talent section and the *Bliss* Soap Awards which draw on teens' fascination with fame and celebrity. On the commercial front *Bliss* goes from strength to strength – it continues to increase its market share and in April carried more ads than *Sugar* for the first time ever.

More!

More! is the UK's biggest selling title for young women. Following on from another successful summer TV campaign, *More!* has gone on to develop exciting new brand extensions. These include the '*More!* Holidays', sponsored this year by Vodafone, and 'Mr *More!* unzipped', the search for a male centrefold, which culminates in a live final at the Clothes Show in December. Other high profile brands that have tapped into *More!*'s success include Garnier who teamed up with the magazine to produce an exclusive in-store promotion in Superdrug during August.

Match the adverts below with the magazines in which they appeared.

You can tell something about the gender, age, leisure pursuits and musical tastes of a magazine's target audience by the advertisements it prints. All the adverts below were taken from three magazines:

▸ *Woman and Home*
▸ *Red*
▸ *CD:UK*

Study the adverts and try to match them to the correct magazine.

FEED YOUR PHONE WITH **logo-to-go!**

For a limited period only, get a free 250ml bottle of Tizer or Irn-Bru with every CD chart single you buy.

The Premier Walk-in Bath helps you relax in comfort.

'Gifts to Paradise' HOAR CROSS HALL The health spa resort in a stately home.

JoJo The UK's most comprehensive mail order maternity collection.

Fruit Shoot is a refreshing fruit drink from Robinsons, available in two fantastic flavours!

DON'T MISS THE NEXT ISSUE OF *TV HITS* FREE! T-SHIRT CUSTOMISING KIT!

This is my Mum wearing her favourite outfit: me. Trust Tomy. Tomy carriers are an essential part of every parent's wardrobe.

SHOP FOR CDs IN SHOES YOU CAN'T WALK IN Buy online at bol.com

Choose a Stannah Stairlift.

'I'm not ready for a bus pass. I'm not under the weather. So why do I take vitamins?' **Centrum**. A complete multimineral–multivitamin formula

OLAY'S LATEST AGE-DEFYING SECRET IS ON EVERYONE'S LIPS

Pasta proof. Pizza proof. Passion proof. It's more than a lipstick, it's lipfinity. MAX FACTOR make-up.

Cover of a recent edition of *Company* magazine

Target markets

Magazine editors need a clear idea of the kinds of people they are hoping to attract and retain as readers. They also need to have a clear idea of the kinds of material that this target market likes to read.

In its promotional literature to potential advertisers, *Company* magazine ('for the freedom years') defines its target market as follows:

Profile		Social grade	%	Age	%
Adult readership	614,000	AB	20	15–19	19
Women readership	550,000	ABC1	71	20–24	31
		C2	17	25–34	34
		DE	12	35–44	10
				45+	6

To appeal to this kind of reader, the magazine projects a 'hip', fresh image with features and articles that are slick, entertaining and tongue-in-cheek.

Analysis of *Smash Hits*

The following case study tries to show you how to use the topics suggested above to analyse a magazine.

THE COVER

The title tells you that the magazine concentrates on very popular music. A hit is a record that has sold well and a 'smash hit' is one which is extremely popular. In case the reader is in any doubt, the description 'THE WORLD'S GREATEST POP MAG!' emphasises the point.

The **style of print** (typography) and the way it is italicised with the letters running into each other plus exclamation mark after *Smash* suggests movement and excitement. The letters *-sh!* are printed in a different colour and hint at secrecy – the magazine has a supplement called 'sneak', which offers 'all this week's juicy gossip'. The Internet address near the barcode indicates to you the magazine is up-to-date, while the lower-case letters in the title suggest informality.

The main image of the cover is a group shot of the members of Blue looking directly at the reader, with the accompanying text promising revelations about them – 'Find out what really turns Blue on'. The specific questions, 'Who's desperate for a date?', 'Which lad dreams of joining S Club?', and 'Who wants an alien baby?' show that the magazine is trying to appeal mainly to teenage girls.

The cover tempts the reader with the promise of excitement and interest inside. Here, the topics are fun ('We force Daniel Bedingfield to eat rattlesnake'); gossip ('We want to give Gareth a makeover'/'Listen in on Misteeq's girlie chat'); fame ('Whose mum is this? Meet the mummies behind the stars'); and sex ('Blazin' Hot – Get your sexy Kenzie poster now!').

THE EDITORIAL

You can usually work out from the editorial what relationship the magazine is trying to establish with its readers. In this issue, the editorial has been written by 'Lisa':

> 'Every pop star we ever speak to at *Smash Hits* says the same thing – their mums are the most important people in their lives. So, in honour of Mother's Day, we've decided to pay a special tribute to the mums behind the stars. Which is why you'll find various celebs telling us why their mums rock on page 46. (Even better, those mums return the favour by revealing everything about their little cherub's teddy bear jumpers and toy monkeys.)
>
> 'What's more, to give the pop mums an afternoon off, we've taken Liberty X ice-skating, played table football with Blue and gone BMXing with Busted. We've even cooked Daniel Bedingfield his tea – giant caterpillars and ant mash – and kept the Kittens quiet by locking them in our Big Mother house. Mum's the word...'

The tone here is conversational and personal, with the writer addressing the reader as 'you' and using everyday words such as 'celebs' and 'mums'. In keeping with the contents of the magazine, it suggests that females are mature and males immature. Mums are 'important people', while male pop stars are called 'little cherubs'.

THE VISUAL IMAGES

The images are almost exclusively of pop stars, with a mixture of posed, publicity shots and more natural, 'off guard' shots. Males and females seem to be represented differently. There are posters and publicity shots of young male pop stars which are included because, as the cover suggests, they are 'sexy' or 'hot'. However, there are also many pictures of young males being 'boyish' – doing tricks on BMX bikes, messing about while playing table football and eating caterpillars. Females, however, are portrayed drinking wine on a night out, drinking coffee in an elegant house and being glamorous.

THE STORIES

A section in *Smash Hits* called 'Planet Pop' has 'gossip, laughs, news, stars, interviews and loads of stupid stuff'.

It starts with a page about Pink, pointing out that she won the Best International Female award at the BRITS. In keeping with the main tone of the magazine, the story emphasises female success and achievement:

> 'She's an inspiration. Pink sings about stuff that affects us all – like divorcing parents and low self-esteem.'

Opposite: Cover of a recent issue of *Smash Hits* magazine

Notice how the writer is assuming that the reader is young and probably insecure. The story also picks out a 'dangerous' quality:

> '...shocking crowds by making dancers dressed as the Queen's guards strip off on stage ... Pink acts like a real rocker.'

However, Pink's serious side is also emphasised:

> 'Pink owns two dogs and two rats and is a regular worker for PETA (People for the Ethical Treatment of Animals). She once banned anybody wearing fur from a gig in New York.'

There is a double-page spread of 'reality' shots of pop stars, headlined: 'A sneaky peek at the crazy peeps of pop.' The candid pictures have comic-style speech bubbles and invite the reader to be amused at stars breaking wind, giving 'V' signs, being badly dressed and adopting silly poses.

These two features (Pink and the 'sneaky peek') represent two attitudes to celebrities – they must be both special and ordinary.

Most of the other features in the magazine are in the form of celebrity quotes. The commonest topic is relationships. Blue talk about 'the worst thing a girl can do on a date' – look tarty or have chipped nail varnish, apparently. Lee and Duncan complain about not being able to get girls:

> 'I'll be one of those tragic blokes who never finds the love of their life.'

Daniel Bedingfield is asked if he has ever 'copped off with a fan'. The girls of Mis-Teeq talk about their wedding plans. Su-Elise says:

> 'I was the first to get engaged, but I haven't sorted anything out yet. But when I get married I want the lot – a huge wedding and a puffy dress that makes me look like a princess.'

THE ADVERTS

You can learn something about the magazine's audience by the kind of advertising it attracts. *Smash Hits* contains adverts for the following:

Health
- Always Ultra pads
- Clearasil

Music
- Mis-Teeq
- Ja Rule and Ashanti
- Woolworths for chart singles
- I Luv *Smash Hits* – album
- Kelly Rowland and S Club tour dates
- Mariah Carey
- Nas
- Atomic Kitten

Mobile phones
- Logos and tones – several pages

Others
- A film poster for *Blue Crush*
- GoPlay TV
- Aimhigher – a government scheme to encourage people to go into further education
- Coca-Cola
- *J17* magazine

These adverts seem to be aimed at young teenagers, especially girls, who have middle-of-the-road pop music tastes, shop at Woolies and use mobile phones frequently.

THE MAGAZINE OWNERS

This is how the EMAP website describes *Smash Hits* to potential advertisers:

> … The magazine continues to be one of EMAP's most innovative brands, providing multimedia solutions that no other media owner can offer. New cross-media firsts with OXY and Smarties on TV, radio and in the magazine itself testify to the vibrancy of the Smash Hits brand. In fact the magazine has the fastest growing advertiser base in the teen market.

This shows the importance of selling an audience to potential advertisers. The media owner first produces something that attracts a very specific audience, in this case teenagers, and then sells space in its product to those advertisers who want to sell products or services to that audience. Media owners can also arrange joint promotions with manufacturers to advertise both the magazine and the manufacturer's product together.

MAKING THE MEDIA — **Design and produce a magazine cover**

Decide what your **target audience** *will be in terms of gender, age, interests and tastes in music.*

▸ *Interview some people who fit the image of your target audience.*
▸ *Find out which celebrities appeal to them and what things they like to read in magazines.*

Choose a fellow student (male or female) and invent a celebrity character for them.

▸ *Produce a short biography (story of their life) for him/her.*
▸ *Decide what sort of an image you want your 'celebrity' to have.*
▸ *Work out with him or her what style of clothes, facial expression, posture and setting would best convey that image to the reader. Take a few photographs in different poses. Choose one of the pictures and make this the basis for your front cover.*

Make up a title for your magazine and select or design the kind of font which would go with it.

Make up a few story headlines for articles inside your magazine.

Think up a realistic free offer (posters, CDs, videos, etc.).

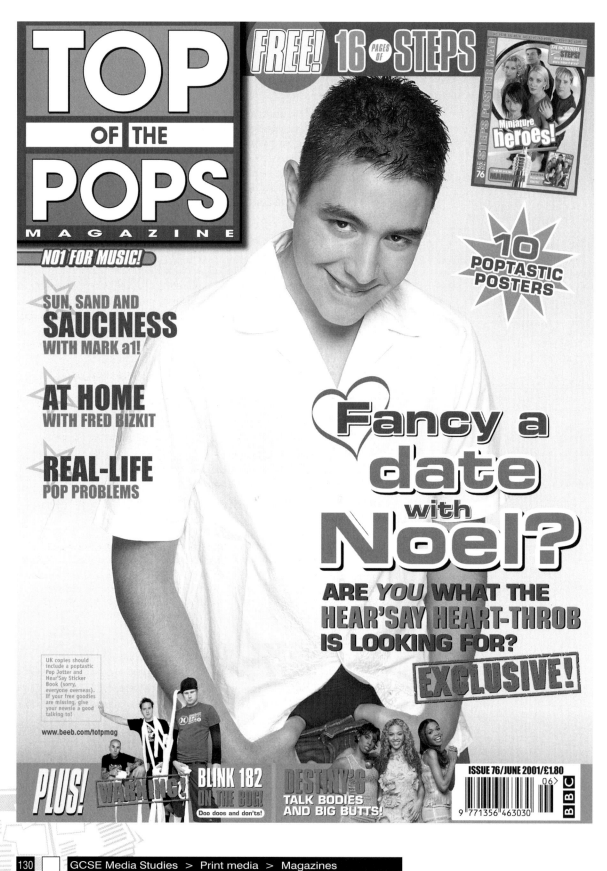

TOP OF THE POPS
MAGAZINE
NO1 FOR MUSIC!

FREE! 16 PAGES OF STEPS

Miniature heroes!

10 POPTASTIC POSTERS

SUN, SAND AND **SAUCINESS** WITH MARK a1!

AT HOME WITH FRED BIZKIT

REAL-LIFE POP PROBLEMS

Fancy a date with Noel?

ARE *YOU* WHAT THE HEAR'SAY HEART-THROB IS LOOKING FOR?

EXCLUSIVE!

UK copies should include a poptastic Pop Jotter and Hear'Say Sticker Book (sorry, everyone overseas). If your free goodies are missing, give your newsie a good talking to!

www.beeb.com/totpmag

PLUS!

WARNING!

BLINK 182 ON THE BOG! Doo doos and don'ts!

DESTINY'S TALK BODIES AND BIG BUTTS!

ISSUE 76/JUNE 2001/£1.80

06>

9 771356 463030

B|B|C

Decide how to position this on the page to attract readers' attention but not to distract attention from the main image.

Produce the finished version of the cover.

*Write an **evaluation** of your cover.*

▸ *How did you conduct research into your target audience?*

▸ *Explain how you chose your 'celebrity' and how you created an image for him/her. How effective was your final cover in attracting interest from your target audience? What improvements would you make for another edition?*

For advice on how to write evaluations, see page 51.

Exam practice ▪▪▪▪▪▪▪▪▪

Printed text analysis

1   Look carefully at the front cover of *Top of the Pops Magazine* and then answer the following questions:

    a   What do you think is the genre of this publication? Give reasons for your answer.

    b   Comment on the choice of celebrity and say what target audience his picture might appeal to.

    c   What do his facial expression and body language suggest?

    d   How does the text that goes with the picture encourage certain readers to look inside the magazine? What other enticements to buy the magazine are there in terms of content and gifts?

2   Choose three items which can be found inside the magazine. Briefly explain why they have been selected.

    a   Briefly describe the layout and design of the cover.

    b   How has the photograph been used to attract an audience?

    c   You are required to design a front cover for a new teenage magazine.

        i   Suggest a title.

        ii   Choose a celebrity who will feature on the cover and justify your choice.

        iii Design a layout for the cover.

        iv   Write notes to explain your layout and design.

        v   Suggest an outline for an article to appear in the magazine.

Comics

>> *This chapter covers:*

- comic conventions in *The Simpsons*
- information on signs, stereotypes and framing in comics
- how to analyse juvenile comics
- comic history
- pre-production exercise in comic conventions
- making a comic story
- exam practice.

Comic conventions

'The Simpsons is one of the most subtle pieces of propaganda around in the cause of sense, humility and virtue.'

Rowan Williams,
Archbishop of
Canterbury, 2002.

Scott McCloud begins his fascinating book *Understanding Comics – The Invisible Art* with these words:

'Comics were those bright, colorful magazines filled with bad art, stupid stories and guys in tights. I read **real** books naturally. I was much too old for comics! But when I was in 8th grade, a friend of mine (who was a lot smarter than I was) convinced me to give comics another look and lent me his collection. Soon I was **hooked**. … I felt there was something lurking in comics...something that had never been done. Some kind of hidden **power**.'

The case study and activities below may help you discover that hidden power.

You can see a variety of comic conventions in the extracts from *The Simpsons* comic. Some of the terminology is similar to that used in analysing moving pictures and photography.

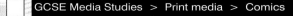

Signs and symbols

In a static, silent medium like comics the problems of indicating sound, movement and state of mind have been addressed by developing a series of signs and symbols. Here are some examples:

Above: Cartoon signs and symbols

Stock characters and stereotypes

Cartoons have to communicate economically and quickly, so certain stock characters and settings have developed. The images are readily recognised by readers familiar with comics even though they are not realistic, for example:

- a burglar is depicted wearing a hooped jumper and a mask, possibly shining a torch and carrying a bag marked 'SWAG'
- a prisoner wears a uniform with arrows on it
- a desert island is shown by a tiny piece of land with a single palm tree on it and a stranded sailor in tattered clothes.

Below: Cartoon stereotypes

The Simpsons: comic conventions

You can see a variety of comic conventions in these extracts from *The Simpsons* comic. Some of the terminology used is similar to that used in the analysis of moving pictures and photography.

All the pictures are contained in **frames** which are sometimes placed inside other frames.

The first frame is an **establishing frame** to show where Lisa is – in her room at home. The details tell you that she has been looking through books and writing a letter.

In the picture are two **speech balloons**. One with a curved 'tail' pointing outside the frame contains words spoken by Lisa's mother downstairs. The other contains Lisa's response.

A cat is on top of a bookcase and **movement lines** show that it is reaching down to a book.

In the next frame a **change in time** is shown by the clock face. The face itself has been **animated** (brought to life) with two eyes. Lisa's closed eyes and the 'Z' sounds show that she is alseep and snoring. Movement lines show that the cat is falling. The frames within a frame are a **flashback** to the moments before Lisa fell asleep.

The **absurdity** of the change of the clock face in the next frame shows that anything goes in comics. The movement lines show that the cat has fallen, knocking the book on to Lisa's head in the process. **Sound effects** are shown with the word

BONK! (the book hitting Lisa), the letters MMMROWWW! (the cat screeching) and the ZZZZ on Lisa's left, indicating a truncated snore.

This is an example of the **compression of time and action** into a single image.

In this frame the insets are **flashforwards** to show what happens when Lisa wakes. In the middle frame the artist has drawn the scene from the same angle but slightly further away and has shown a **different angle** of Lisa's face. In the third frame she has a different **perspective** on the room and is shown in silhouette.

Framing

Frames are basic to comic technique and they can be used (or even not used) creatively, as in these examples:

Frame 1
A jagged outline gives a feeling of tension and torment.

Frame 2
The long panel suggests height, while the small panels are positioned to create a tumbling effect.

Frame 3
The figure seems to be breaking out of the panel, suggesting power and action.

Frame 4
No frame suggests unlimited space.

Frame 5
The door becomes the panel and suggests a confined space.

Frame 6
The cloud-like shape suggests a dream or a fantasy.

READING THE MEDIA

Study three issues of a children's comic then complete the activities below.

*Explain how you **know** that the publication in question is a comic.*

▶ *How can you tell children's comics from other sorts of comic, such as fantasy, science fiction, horror, war, adventure, superhero, romance, educational or sport?*

*Describe the main **characters** in terms of age, gender, activities and attitudes.*

▶ *What happens to '**posh**' or '**soft**' kids? What physical characteristics do they have and what do they wear? How are they mocked and made to look foolish?*

▶ *How are bullies represented? Are they always male? What particular physical characteristics do they have?*

▶ *How are authority figures portrayed? What makes them seem foolish? Do they assert their authority successfully or are they ignored?*

*Is there any pattern to the **stories**?*

▶ *Do the main characters challenge older people?*

▶ *How do they respond to authority figures such as parents and teachers?*

▶ *Is there a pattern of their being clever, witty and cheeky?*

*What sorts of **humour** are there? Describe three examples of visual jokes.*

*Describe three examples of **violent conduct**. What are the consequences of these?*

*Describe an example of **physical distortion** and its consequences.*

Comics: the target market

When you analyse a comic title you should look at several issues, some from the past as well as contemporary ones if possible. Try to find out from the publisher what sort of readers the comic is aiming to attract. Ask the publisher for a free media pack containing the kind of information that is normally sent to advertisers.

This is the kind of information you can find:

▶ *The Beano and its stablemate the Dandy are the two most widely read juvenile comics in Britain, with a combined readership of over a million.*

▶ *The Beano's main target group is 7–14-year-olds. One third of its readers are girls.*

▶ *15% of Beano readers are 14 or over.*

A typical Calamity James story from the *Beano*

> *For the benefit of advertisers, the* Beano *keeps detailed records of the tastes and preferences of its 7–10-year-old readers, including how many of them:*

- *play with hand-held games machines*
- *own a bike*
- *eat chocolate*
- *visit theme parks*
- *have money in a building society*
- *choose the newest trainers*
- *visit burger bars*
- *keep a pet.*

It also records how many of its 11–14-year-old readers:

- *play video games*
- *have a mountain bike*
- *enjoy swimming*
- *visit cinemas*
- *buy CDs*
- *eat up to four bars of chocolate per week*
- *choose the newest trainers.*

Analysis of a Calamity James story

Genre and narrative conventions

One of the main conventions of the children's comic is that **anything goes**. The events do not have to be realistic. A mad millionaire can wear underpants filled with mushy peas, James's feet can become larger than the rest of his body and his hair can turn into fire. But we know that in the next edition of the *Beano* he will be as good as new.

In Calamity James stories, the main character is **one-dimensional**. He does not have any complexities, nor does he develop. He has a single main characteristic, which is that painful misfortunes happen to him whenever he tries to do anything.

As with several children's stories the main character has a **pet companion**, in this case 'James's small but perfectly formed lemming chum, Alexander'. The convention is that this pet can talk and move like a human being. The lemming is a faithful and long-suffering companion who avoids the worst of the catastrophes that befall James and gives him advice and help.

Each Calamity James story forms a **basic pattern** of challenge (which can be simply trying to do something quite normal), followed by surreal confusion or complication which leads to a painful conclusion.

In the story opposite, the challenge for James is to buy some trendy trainers so that the other kids won't taunt him. A mad millionaire gives him money to buy the trainers, but a rhinoceros competing in the round-the-world roller-skating championship skates over them and ruins them. His feet swell to an impossible size and he has to wear old boxes instead.

Other Calamity James stories often tend to follow a similar pattern, as these two examples show:

- *Story 1:* James attends an athletics meeting, only to find himself in a seat with a 'very strong extremely dangerous spring' in it. He is hurled towards the water jump, only to be hit by the shot propelled by a vast female shot-putter. She is so enraged that she uses James as a substitute shot.

- *Story 2:* James wants to join in a New Year's party, but is thrown out of a nursery and an old people's home where parties are going on. Then he skids on some ice, hits a tree and lands up in hospital. There is a party going on here, but he can't enjoy it as he is encased in bandages and told not to eat or drink for seven days.

Values

The values of the comic's writer are apparent in some of the details. He often seems to **satirise consumerism**. Here his two teenagers, who value trendy trainers so much, are depicted in absurd clothes and appear ridiculous when they worship James because he has new trainers. The trendy trainers are themselves ridiculously over the top, with a built-in stereo CD player and miniaturised colour satellite TV.

Interpretations

Different readers will find different meanings in the Calamity James stories. Some readers, like critic George Gale *(see below)*, might take these misfortunes as a cruel punishment for James who is poor, ugly and a little stupid.

Others might see themselves in many of his situations and see the stories as a comment on the blows that life dishes out to us. Despite his misfortunes, James never gives up trying to lead a normal life, while his chum Alexander Lemming is completely loyal.

The influence of comics

What sort of influence do comics have on their readers? Find older people who have read comics and ask them how they have been influenced and what they remember about the comics they read when they were younger.

Here is an example of the kind of criticism levelled at comics:

> *While violence is the main feature of these children's comics, the systematic destruction of the English language runs it a close second. The blows, falls, shrieks, crunches, etc., are accompanied by a proliferation of non-words … A survey of these and similar comics would show that each week children are invited to laugh at people who are fat, deformed, handicapped or ugly, especially when pain is being inflicted. This is accompanied by crude, ugly language. Such a regular diet can do nothing but harm children.'*
>
> *George Gale*

Use this as a starting point for forming your own opinions of the characters, use of language, and the effect that comics have on you. Alternatively, interview regular readers of comics and record their reactions to Gale's point of view.

Characteristics of juvenile comics

- Stories are simple and full of action.
- There is one main character.
- Characters are simple, not complex.
- The characters who make things happen are children – or behave like children.
- Characters can do impossible things.
- Characters who are 'soft', 'nice' or the teacher's pet usually suffer.
- When characters suffer they recover or appear unchanged at the start of the next episode.
- Drawings are simplified rather than lifelike.
- Most natural laws can be broken.

Brief history of comics

There is no agreement about when comics started, but if you accept the definition of a comic as a story told in pictures, then the history of comics could go back as far as the Bayeaux Tapestry, which tells in pictorial form the story of the Battle of Hastings in 1066. Possible precursors of modern comics can be found in a number of unlikely places:

- In the Middle Ages, stained-glass windows in churches told Biblical stories.
- Following the discovery of printing in the 1400s (the Chinese had invented it hundreds of years earlier), it became possible for 'picture stories' on religious themes to be widely distributed throughout Europe. *The Tortures of Saint Erasmus* (1460) was one popular example.
- In the eighteenth century, the artist William Hogarth produced satirical paintings and engravings which tell a simplified comic story.
- Something closer to the modern comic was produced in the mid-1800s by Rodolphe Topffer, who combined words and pictures and introduced panel borders in his sequences of cartoons.

The twentieth-century comic

In the early twentieth century, there were woodcut novels in the UK and Belgium which could be classed as comics, but it was not until the 1930s that comics as we know them today began to become popular.

In June 1938, Superman first appeared in Action Comics – the first of the comic-book superheroes. Jack Kirby introduced a new style of action drawings: 'To emphasise the energetic movement of my characters I tore them out of the panels. I made them jump all over the page.' Kirby made fights last for a page or more rather than just a couple of frames.

Comics from the late 1930s through to the 1940s abounded with superheroes and fight sequences. Comics were ideal for portraying the activities of superheroes. Books could not match the immediate visual appeal of comics, and films had not yet developed the special effects to make superhero activity believable.

The comics code

In 1950 in the USA, the Comics Code Authority enforced strict regulations governing the content of comics:

- no corrupt police or politicians
- no sexy females
- no blood or gore
- nothing to show criminal methods
- no walking dead
- no torture
- no unnecessary knife or gun play
- no titles with the words 'weird', 'crime', 'horror' or 'terror'.

This was followed by a huge reduction in the number of comics on the market.

n 1964, the formation of comic fan clubs led to new production and marketing practices, with smaller print runs being sold to established groups of readers. As a result, fewer copies were left unsold.

The 1970s and 1980s saw the emergence of counterculture or 'underground' comics. Produced partly in defiance of the Comics Code Authority, these were rebellious and unconventional. Many were only produced for a few issues. One that was very influential was *Mad*, which deliberately set out to shock by attacking traditional middle-class values.

This influence spread to the UK and Europe, where comics had generally been produced only for the juvenile market, eventually leading to the publication of 'adult comics' such as *Viz*.

Below: A scene from a *Dr Strange* comic which shows characters 'breaking out' of the panels

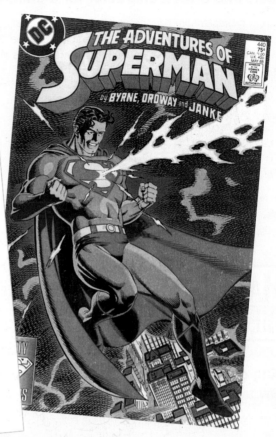

'As a high school student, I thought that someday I might become a reporter, and I had crushes on several attractive girls who either didn't know I existed or didn't care... It occurred to me – what if I was really terrific? What if I had something really special going for me, like jumping over buildings or throwing cars around or something like that? Then maybe they would notice me. That night when all the thoughts were coming to me, the concept came to me that Superman could have a dual identity, and that in one of his identities he would be meek and mild, as I was, and wear glasses, as I do. The heroine, who I figured would be a girl reporter, would think he was some sort of a worm yet she would be crazy about this Superman character ... In fact she was real wild about him, and the big inside joke was that the fellow she was crazy about was also the fellow she loathed.'

Jerry Siegel (Superman's creator)

Using comic conventions

Produce the following comic frames:

Draw a frame using movement lines to show Calamity James being propelled through the air by a faulty spring or an irate shot putter.

Draw a frame with movement lines and sound effects to show James landing in a pond.

Draw frames to show Lisa Simpson looking (a) downcast, (b) scared, and (c) happy.

Draw single frames using symbols to show:

▸ *someone in love*
▸ *someone with a bright idea*
▸ *someone who is puzzled*
▸ *someone who is dreaming of food.*

Create and draw a character for a children's comic.

Give your character some distinctive physical characteristics and way of dressing. Invent and draw a pet for the character. Give the character a single characteristic which will allow you to write many storylines around the same theme. For instance, he/she:

▶ *can become invisible*
▶ *is able to fly*
▶ *can see into the future*
▶ *can't stop eating*
▶ *is always getting into mischief*
▶ *is accident-prone.*

Write two or three storylines for your character based on the pattern of challenge or problem, two or three consequences or complications and a resolution or solution.

Using one idea from the pre-production exercise, draw a complete story in 10–20 frames.

Describe your target audience.

▶ *Interview members of your target audience, showing them a rough draft of your story and make notes on their reactions.*

Describe other comic stories which are already published and explain briefly how yours will be different. Which publication would your story be most suitable for and why?

Complete the final version after taking account of the reactions.
Write an evaluation of your story.

▶ *Describe the research you did, which can include looking at comics with similar sorts of stories. State what problems you encountered and how you solved them.*

For advice on how to write evaluations, see page 51.

Guidelines

▶ *Comic scripts are usually produced at twice 'finished' size (i.e. the size they eventually appear in comics).*
  If you use speech bubbles, it is easier to do the text before drawing the bubble.
  Try to vary the angles from which you view your characters.
  Vary the size of the images.
  Use occasional close-ups, especially if you want to show feelings.

Exam practice

Choose the cover pages from two contrasting comics (e.g. an action/adventure comic and a children's comic). Study these carefully and then answer these questions:

1   Choose a character from the covers and briefly describe their character as suggested by the image.

2   How do these two covers try to attract an audience?

3   **a**   Choose a title for a story that might appear in one of the comics.
    b   Draw the main character and briefly describe his or her characteristics.
    c   Write a brief outline of the story.
    d   Write brief notes to explain why an audience would be interested in the character and the story.

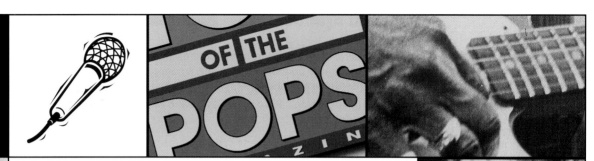

Chapter 12 — Popular music

Popular music

>> *This chapter covers:*
- how to analyse different kinds of pop music
- a case study on the blues genre
- how new performers are identified and marketed
- the portrayal of performers in videos and promotional material
- links between music, radio and the record industry
- the reporting of pop music
- how to devise an image for a band and prepare a promotional campaign

 **READING THE MEDIA**  **Analysing pop music**

You should aim to be able to describe a type (genre) of music in some detail. Try to:

▸ *find out how the style originated*
▸ *describe the style of singing*
▸ *state what instruments are used and the sound they make*
 describe the topics of the lyrics
 identify the main performers
 discover whether there is any distinctive pattern to the music and the words
 find out whether or not the form changes over time.

Case Study:
The blues genre

The birth of the blues

The blues **genre** had its origins amongst the African American enslaved population of the southern USA at the beginning of the twentieth century. It developed from work songs or shouts, and featured mainly a solo voice and an instrumental accompaniment.

Country blues

The earliest blues were known as **country** or **delta blues** because they originated in the Mississippi Delta in the USA. They were sung by vagabond singer/guitarists or harmonica players who played wherever African American people congregated. The singers earned money in the same way as buskers. Many of the early singers were physically disabled and could not earn wages by labouring so turned to music instead.

Blues legend Muddy Waters

The style of a country blues singer, Son House, as described by folklorist Alan Lomax

'Hitch up my black pony, saddle up my bay mare,' he sang, his words conjuring up nights of coupling in the tropical heat of Mississippi. His voice, guttural and hoarse with passion, ripping apart the surface of the music like his tractor-driven deep plough ripped apart the wet black earth in the springtime, making the sap of the earth song run, while his powerful, work-hard hands snatched strange chords out of the steel strings … And with him, the sorrow of the blues... Son's whole body wept, as with his eyes closed, the tendons in his powerful neck standing out with the violence of his feeling and his brown face flushing, he sang in an awesome voice the 'Death Letter Blues'.

from *The History of the Blues* by Francis Davis (Secker and Warburg, 1995)

Say you can never tell, what some of these women's mind,
Said you can never tell what some of these women's mind,
Yeah, keep on huggin' and kissin' you and treatin' you all the time.
Said I went home this morning 'twixt nine-thirty and ten,
Said I went home this morning 'twixt nine-thirty and ten,
Yeah I met that woman's second man, right right back in my den.
Said a woman's just like a dollar, dollar go from hand to hand,
Said a woman's just like a dollar, dollar go from hand to hand,
Yeah, some these low down women just run from man to man.

Lyrics of *Jivin' Woman Blues* by Blind Boy Fuller

Music and lyrics

Originally, blues lyrics were in rhyming three-line verses, the first line being repeated.

The words of the song on the left are typical of the blues, in that they are about deceit and sex rather than romantic love. Other common **themes** in the blues are travel, poverty, rejection and loneliness.

There is a standard **chord progression** in blues based on the three major chords of a scale, and the melody is sweetly mournful because of the characteristic 'blue notes', which are flattened thirds, fifths and sevenths.

Different styles of blues have developed over the years. One is the **bottleneck** style of guitar playing, which involves 'stopping' the strings using a metal bar or the neck of a glass bottle, to produce a sound like a voice moaning.

Changing styles

The blues changed over time, as all styles must if they are to survive. As blacks moved into towns in search of work, male and female blues singers started to perform with piano accompaniment or small jazz combos. Singers such as Bessie Smith and Louis Armstrong performed in bars and dance halls.

Electric blues

After World War II, the centre of blues activity moved to Chicago and **electric blues** with amplified guitars became popular. The singer Muddy Waters (see page 147) became well known for this more urban style. He and others influenced white singers such as Elvis Presley and thus the start of **rock and roll**. Waters toured Britain in 1958 and inspired a whole generation of British musicians who later became innovators in rock music.

Further study

Other forms of music genres which you could study in this way are:

- hip hop
- hard rock
- jazz
- country and western
- rap
- punk
- reggae
- soul
- new age.

READING THE MEDIA

Analysing performers

Choose a pop musician, singer or band to study in detail, using the questions and guidelines below.

*Describe the **image** of the performer or performers (includes dress, actions and posture while performing, types of music, style of speaking and lifestyle).*

*In what **settings** are the performers photographed and how significant are these settings? (For instance, rock bands are often pictured in 'mean' urban settings, while dance acts are photographed in studios where their clothes, hairstyles and make-up can be emphasised.)*

*How **genuine** are the performers and how far have they been primed to behave in certain ways? How can you tell?*

*Try to find **publicity material** for the performers you are studying and if possible find **evidence** of how their image is created.*

*Find examples of how the image of the performers you are analysing is spread and reinforced by **publicity in pop magazines.** Look at interviews and list the kinds of information that you are presented with in **magazines**. Ask what sort of audience the writer is addressing in terms of age group and gender (e.g. pre-teenage girls).*

The making of a band

Here is how 'The official inside story of Hear'Say' (disbanded in October 2002) describes the band's first all-day photo-shoot:

On a dark, damp Tuesday in early February Danny, Myleene, Kym, Noel and Suzanne gather together for their first all-day photo shoot. The band's manager Chris Herbert is there, along with promotions and A and R people from their record company Polydor.

There's the stylist Juice and her assistant hairstylist Martin Gayle and his team, the make-up artist for the shoot and photographer Sandrine Dulermo and her team. And, to top it all, the *Popstars* production crew are all there to document the first time the newly styled *Popstars* band has ever been seen together.

The transformation is striking. Suzanne loves her new waist-length hair and glamorous look, while Kim has a vivid red streak in her fringe. In the freezing studio, only Danny is not feeling the cold (in fact he's spent so much time next to the brazier full of flames that he's boiling) and Noel's feet are killing him, as they've been squashed into a pair of trainers two sizes too small. Myleene, as ever, is taking it all in her stride.

It's really hard work and the band are constantly surrounded by people, but they know that what will come out of the long day is the image that will introduce HEAR'SAY to the world.

from Popstars – The Making of a Band
by Maria Malone (Trafalgar Square)

▸ *For instance, in* Top of the Pops Magazine *(see page 130), the questions that form the basis of the interview with Noel from the band Hear'Say are posed from the point of view of a female teenager who would like to meet Noel. The female audience has been directly addressed by the invitation on the cover under a picture of a shy-looking Noel:*

> *'Fancy a date with Noel? Are you what the Hear'Say heart-throb is looking for?'*

Inside, the questions are along the lines of:

– *'What's the most important quality that we, as your date, should possess?'*
– *'How would you make your romantic intentions clear to us?'*

Then the questions become more about sex than romance:

– *'How far would you go on a first date?'*
– *'How many dates before things get ruder?'*

Gradually the image of the singer changes from little shy boy into something rather more suggestive.

▸ *Look for **newspaper coverage** at the time of the release of an album. Usually this is based on an interview and supported with a photograph. To be a musician or singer is not enough: artists must be able to communicate across the media. They must also have something interesting to say. They may be encouraged by publicity staff to be deliberately controversial and provocative, to make up incidents, and to exaggerate stories about themselves.*

An example of newspaper coverage is given on page 150.

The Quiet Boys

Starsailor tell Stephanie Merritt why they'll never be Oasis

It seems the new century has bred a new kind of rock star, politely serious young men who would rather discuss chord sequences than destroy hotel rooms, even if they do have slightly scruffy hair.

Often loosely grouped under the reductive label 'New Acoustic Movement' (with the slogan 'Quiet is the new Loud') they include Travis, Coldplay, Ed Harcourt and, most recently, Starsailor, hailed by NME as 'the best new band in Britain' on the release of their first single 'Fever'.

'The turning point for me was when I realised I could never be Liam Gallagher or Tim Burgess because I was too shy,' explains their frontman, guitarist and song writer, James Walsh, smiling apologetically from beneath a shaggy fringe. That's when I turned to people like Neil Young and Joni Mitchell, because they seemed like nice, down-to-earth people who wrote exceptional songs, rather than someone like Liam who wanted to be put on a pedestal and be a star.'

Observer Review *23.9.01*

© *The Observer*

---

*Find examples of the activities of pop music performers **making the news**.*

▷ *The tabloid press have begun to devote more space to pop musicians, not just in the music or review pages but in their news coverage too. The popular tabloids have a huge readership, and a story about a pop star can appear in the morning and be talked about all over the country by teatime.*

Publicity

When you look at pop music magazines, you should be aware that most of the material you are reading is provided by marketing or **publicity departments** of record companies.

Here is an example about Nicky of Westlife:

'I went out on Sunday with all my friends to play golf,' *says Nicky of Westlife*. 'The record company bought us all golf clubs for Christmas. Me and my friend Shaun played against my other mate Paul, who is absolutely brilliant. We won in the end though – we took £20 each off him, ha-ha.'

He (or more likely his ghost writer) goes on:

> 'The main thing I'm enjoying about being back is my mam's cooking!
> If I don't cook, then my mam has a traditional Irish fry-up waiting for me!
> There are sausages, rashers, eggs, black pudding, fried bread and a big
> cup of tea. I can't move after it, I'm so stuffed!'

And there's more:

> 'Myself and Georgina have just bought a house, so I've been out buying
> furniture and wallpapering. It's more stress than being in the band –
> you end up cracking up over paint colours! It's in the country and it's like
> a log cabin, though I'm putting in a pool room, which will be cool!'

Top of the Pops Magazine,
June 2001

The aim of the article seems to be to portray Nicky as both ordinary and exceptional. He likes golf and pool. He has lots of mates, a mam and a partner, and he likes fry-ups. He's just an ordinary feller really – except that he gets a set of golf clubs for a Christmas present and can afford to buy and furnish a log cabin in the country. So he is also different because of his wealth and stardom.

Tabloid journalists are not so much concerned about performances and records, but about 'good stories' concerning **drugs**, **money** and **sex**. Some of them can conduct vendettas against performers and can distort stories and print unflattering pictures. *The Sun's* libelling of Elton John and their 'stalking' of Boy George are notorious examples of hostile press coverage.

READING THE MEDIA — Analyse a pop video

Choose a pop video that you find interesting and analyse it by answering the questions below.

What image is the band/solo performer presenting?

▶ *Look at clothes, hairstyles, posture, facial expressions and gestures.*
▶ *How well does the image go with the settings used in the video?*
▶ *How similar is it to the image of the performer which has already been established?*

*If the video features a **group**, how are the individual members presented? Do they have individual styles and personalities or are they presented as a team, with their similarities highlighted?*

How well does the pace of the editing match the content and mood of the song?

▶ *What different camera angles are used and with what effect? A low angle might emphasise the performer's power or sexuality, whereas a high angle, looking down on the performer, might suggest vulnerability.*

Promotional videos

Image is crucial in promotional videos, and will be determined by the artist negotiating with the A&R staff ('artists and repertoire' – *see below*), the marketing department, the video director and sometimes a stylist.

The **stylist** may work by adapting images found by looking through magazines and old films, or simply by going shopping with the artist and trying out different styles.

The video made by Queen in 1975 based on *Bohemian Rhapsody* is thought to be the first deliberate use of video to **promote a pop single**.

It was the launch of **MTV** (in the USA in 1981), the first 24-hour TV channel devoted exclusively to pop music, which established the video as a vital part of the pop process.

However, makers of pop videos have to work within certain constraints. A pop video has to protect the identity of the act, suit the music of a particular track and keep within the limitations of the artist or performer. The speed at which a video is produced (it normally takes two days) may result in things having to be put together to cover mistakes or to make the best of a bad job. What may look to the viewer like a bold artistic statement may be simply a clever way to solve or cover up a technical problem.

Making a video does not necessarily mean it will be broadcast. During a typical week in the UK in 1990, there were 146 opportunities to place a video. The most airtime was on the ITV *Chart Show*, broadcast on Saturday morning children's TV. The producer of the show estimated that he was offered 50 videos per week, from which he selected about five.

Sometimes there are constraints on video production imposed by MTV, which insists on **fast editing**. Videos are often shown on children's programmes, which means that there are stringent restrictions on portrayal of smoking and sex and violence. For all these reasons, record companies have to think carefully whether to invest money in a video or in touring and other promotional activities.

The structure of a record company

Typically the progress of a band or performer goes like this:

- band/performer signs with record company
- material is developed
- material is recorded
- material is packaged
- material appears in the shops.

Artists and Repertoire (A&R)

These members of staff find music, writers and performers, and decide whether a company should invest in them. They listen to demo tapes, visit clubs and take calls from writers, managers and bands. If they like the material, they need to know if the band has a manager, who writes their material, how permanent their line-up is, who else is showing an interest and if the band have any recorded material.

The questions they ask are:

- Is the act any good?
- Is there an audience for their music?
- Is the band professional?

Sometimes, small independent record companies (**indies**) are used as A&R departments by larger companies. Sometimes they are even bought up by them, as when Polygram bought up Island Records, thus effectively buying U2.

A&R people will work with a newly signed band and discuss their strengths and weaknesses. The material will be analysed for song structure, instrumentation, lyrics and vocal performance. If the artists have difficulty in writing or completing songs, the A&R people will either enlist the help of established songwriters, locate music from back catalogues or commission new songs.

Marketing
People involved in marketing arrange and co-ordinate advertising schedules, organise press and promotion campaigns and are responsible for ensuring product visibility at retail outlets (places where records are sold).

The marketing department has to match the performer to a category which is successful. To do this, it needs videos, press advertisements, and radio and TV appearances, all presenting a clear image. This image, once established, has to be reinforced in posters, concert tickets and stage outfits.

To help the media-buying process, the **target market** has to be established in terms of age, gender and lifestyle. The marketing department has to promote the band or performer through media which the target group is likely to read, see or hear. The timing of publicity campaigns is also crucial.

Getting a record into the charts is vital, and this involves influencing radio producers, DJs and retailers. Once this has been achieved, the marketing becomes a lot easier.

Marketing changes as the population changes. For example, as the number of teenage consumers has declined as a proportion of the population, a growing middle-aged, middle-class market has appeared.

Creative services
This department has to co-ordinate sleeve, poster and advertising design, set designs for tours and video production.

Production
This department has to oversee and arrange the actual manufacturing of the discs, the promotional material, the release of the material and the ordering of stocks.

Sales and distribution
Salespeople take orders from retailers and supply them with records and promotional material.

Indies and majors
Independent or 'indie' record companies usually comprise a group of artists who write their own songs, hire studio time, then record, press, label and

distribute their own records on a small scale. They concentrate on a small group of artists and/or a single genre.

Majors are multinational. They publish, manufacture, distribute and market on a large scale, have a series of labels and a variety of genres. Majors usually have outlets all over the world.

Producers

In the history of pop music, the role of the producer came to the fore as a result of George Martin's work with the Beatles. In the period when the band were concentrating on recording rather than performing live, Martin played an important creative role and was very influential in shaping their distinctive sound.

The producer is actively involved with the selection and arrangement of the artist's material. The producer will be responsible for the final mixing where already recorded instruments and voices are blended together, balanced and multi-tracked, and embellished with effects that determine how a record will sound to the consumer.

Managers

Managers look after the interests of individual performers or bands. This involves negotiating deals with record companies and concert promoters. They support, rather than interfere with, the performer's creativity. They check the venues for live performances for suitability and conditions, and make sure that tours are properly promoted. They work closely with marketing people to make sure that the right markets are being targeted in the right way.

Publishers

Publishers earn their money by controlling the performing and recording rights to songs. Performing rights apply to every piece of music that is broadcast for public consumption. Radio and television companies must log every piece of music they play and pay royalties to the publisher each time the music is played or used. Publishers will aim to get their songs recognised as widely as possible, including in commercials like the Levi adverts of the 1990s.

Promoting records on radio

Radio stations provide one of the most important promotional outlets for popular music. The promotional life of a single is brief. Record companies will 'plug' a single for about three weeks. If it has little airplay in that time, in all probability it will be a commercial failure.

Commercial radio stations tend to have a clearly defined target audience and will always be interested in the kinds of sounds that will attract and keep that audience. They can then 'sell' that audience to advertisers.

There are over 100 independent local radio stations, the vast majority featuring a combination of Top 40/contemporary chart hits, middle-of-the-road/easy listening, classic hits and 'oldies'.

The BBC is different because it is paid for out of the licence fee rather than from advertising revenue. It sees Radio 1 in these terms:

Record industry facts

The Beatles made their first hit, Please Please Me, in a single day.

In terms of ownership, 70% of popular recorded music is produced, manufactured and distributed by **five** major companies:

- **EMI Music Group** (owned by British-based Thorn-EMI)
- **Polygram** (part of the Dutch-based Philips corporation)
- **Sony Music Entertainment** (a division of the Japanese Sony Corporation)
- **Warner Music International** (part of Time-Warner, the largest entertainment corporation in the world)
- the **BMG Music Group** (a subsidiary of the German Bertelsmann group).

Records were originally produced in single (45 rpm) and long-playing (33⅓ rpm) format. In the 1950s and 1960s, the pop market was dominated by singles.

The first record charts were published by the New Musical Express in 1952 (Top 12). This became the Top 20 in 1954.

In the mid-1950s, jukeboxes were brought to the UK from the USA.

In 1958, the four-channel tape recorder was introduced. This enabled musicians to accompany themselves, and the technique of over-dubbing developed as a consequence.

In 1967, The Beatles' Sergeant Pepper album was recorded on two four-track tape recorders and was an early example of the imaginative use of over-dubbing in pop.

In the 1970s, more sophisticated recording machinery became available, with 48 tracks and synthesisers so that keyboards had a wider range of sounds available. The mixing of records involved producers and engineers as well as performers.

In the 1970s, computerised recording techniques were introduced, which meant that sounds could be recorded and stored and then manipulated and modified at will. Studio quality recording can now take place in any location.

Until 1966, the normal practice for a band was to do concert tours for 10 months and then spend a few weeks recording. The Beatles changed that, spending 90% of their time in recording studios.

Pop videos made for TV were initiated by the Beatles and became widely used in the 1970s.

In the mid-1960s, The Beatles wrote their own material. This was highly unusual at the time. Records were, in effect, live performances.

> Radio 1's role is to innovate in popular radio, develop new formats, encourage new talent, play new music. As a publicly funded radio station it has the ability to do all these things and take risks ... I am interested in finding new ways of putting speech into music radio, but not in great slabs of speech.
>
> former Radio 1 Controller Matthew Bannister

This policy has led to an increase in speech on Radio 1 – including record reviews, news programmes, rockumentaries and 'talky bits' in music shows.

On other stations, the tendency is to reduce speech to a minimum in popular music programmes. But Radio 1, which at its peak in the early 1990s was attracting audiences of over 4 million, is the most influential station in terms of promoting records.

Record company promotion staff try to build up a relationship with particular DJs or producers and identify which of them will be receptive to a particular artist. Promotional staff take recordings and information to radio station personnel and may invite them to performances.

DJs themselves are keen to enhance their own reputation and like to become involved with 'discovering' and developing new talent.

New technologies

Technological inventions have changed the nature of popular music in the western world – but the changes have not always been welcomed.

- The introduction of the **microphone** led to complaints from BBC executives about how it led to a decline in 'real singing' and encouraged 'crooning'.
- In the 1960s, folk music audiences complained about the use of electric instruments and **amplification**, and rock critics have condemned 'artificial' disco and dance music for their use of synthesisers.

For hundreds of years, people have argued that new musical technologies are in some way **false** and that they lead to a decline in the skills of music-making. What is being replaced is often seen as more real and authentic.

- As far back as 1611, people were complaining about **loss of musical skills**. The guitar was beginning to replace the lute at that time, and the inquisitor Sebastian de Covarrubias wrote that the guitar was like a cowbell which even 'a stable boy who is not a musician' could play.
- In the late eighteenth century the **piano** was considered a revolutionary music-making machine. It replaced the harpsichord and gave greater dynamic (i.e. loud–soft) contrast, allowing composers and performers a much wider expressive range.

The year 1979 saw the introduction of the **Sony Walkman**, a miniaturised personal tape-player. This invention, along with portable radios and car stereos, changed the way in which pop music was consumed.

The Walkman has allowed individuals to impose their own soundscape on their environment and to **listen to music privately** in a public space.

Rework the image of a band or solo performer which you think needs to be changed.

The image should be presented in publicity material such as posters, CD covers, websites, press releases, etc. You can do this with original drawings and paintings, by cutting and pasting images from magazines or by manipulating computer images.

▸ *Consider facial expressions, hairstyles, clothing, posture, gesture and setting or background. Always give reasons for all your choices or creations.*

▸ *Alternatively, continue the description on page 158 of the many faces of Madonna, describing and illustrating with photos her different images since 1990.*

Devise a publicity campaign for an imaginary band.

Use original artwork, cut and paste photographs or use computer-generated pictures to depict the band.

*Describe the type of **music** the band perform.*

*Describe the target **audience** they are performing for in terms of age, gender, geography, ethnic origin and lifestyle, for example: teenage, mainly girls but some boys; mainly UK audience, but possibly appealing also to North Americans, fun-loving clubbers and party-goers, etc.*

*Work out what magazines and newspaper columns this target group will be likely to read and what TV and radio stations they will be likely to listen to. Write a **press release** about the band to send to these media.*

The press release should contain:

▸ *information about the members of the band*
▸ *a description of the kinds of live performances they give*
▸ *details about where they are performing*
▸ *whether they write their own material*
▸ *what recordings they have made.*

You will find an example of a press release on page 159.

You could also design a CD cover to go with the press release.

The changing face of Madonna

1983 Madonna album
'Mad clank of crucifixes and chains with Madonna showing lots of navel. Lacy tights, stretch skirts and ripped vest tops completed the clashy, manic gypsy look that was soon to be seen on every High Street in the Western world.'

1984 Like a Virgin album
'Fleshy and voluptuous in lashings of white lace with fingerless gloves and swept-up hair, wearing an 'ironic' badge saying Boy Toy. The gaudy prom-queen-from-hell look established Madonna as a serious trendsetter.'

1986 *True Blue* album
'Tiered layers of cloth and more metal than a cutlery drawer, this is the stripped down Madonna, very blonde, very cool. Start of the homage to Marilyn Monroe.'

1987 *You Can Dance* album
'Continuation of the Monroe look. She crops her shoulder-length hair into a shorter style, echoing the screen goddess who has obsessed her since her teens. Time for conical bras, fishnets, corsets, gold lame suits and jewelled bustiers.'

1989 Like a Prayer album
'More stylish than sexy. After a break from pop she went back to her roots with centre-parted, dark, shoulder-length hair. She said it was great to have her own colour back because blondes were not taken seriously. Adopted a hippy look of jewels, jeans, trouser suits and patterned waistcoats.'

1990 *I'm Breathless* album
'Return of the peroxide vamp. Performing a song at the Oscars she could hardly look more like her late heroine Miss Monroe, swathed in diamonds and a white fur stole. Either that or she was a Betty Boop with cupid bow lips.'

The changing image of Madonna during the 1980s, as described by a *Sunday Mirror* supplement

Victoria Beckham: A sample press release

Popstar, media myth, Spice Girl, author, footballer's wife, style icon, mother – this we know. But who is the real Victoria Beckham? Her debut solo album is possibly the biggest insight yet – full of clues, great tunes and intriguing lyrics, it goes a long way to answering the questions.

VICTORIA BECKHAM Debut Solo Album 'Victoria Beckham' released on 1 October 2001

The album kicks off with a winner – her debut single **'Not Such An Innocent Girl'**. Here good girl meets bad girl in a futuristic variation on *West Side Story*. The groove-laden third track **'That Kind of Girl'** has the memorable line 'drinking champagne out of paper cups'. 'That's very me and David,' says Victoria.

R and B music has featured in much of the Spice Girls' work and you can hear the same influence in **'Victoria Beckham'**. The sophisticated sound suits her down to the ground, especially on **'I Wish'** and **'Watcha Talkin' Bout'**.

Victoria's writing talents show up in 9 out of the 12 album tracks. She showed her writing talent in *Learning to Fly*, her autobiography, published by Penguin Books in September. The immensely likeable Victoria shows herself a dab hand at writing and bares her soul in the process.

There are some superb ballads on the album, especially **'Unconditional Love'** and **'I.O.U.'**, written for David, 'as I feel I owe him everything'. Also very moving is **'Every Part of Me'** which features Brooklyn, who spent a lot of time in the studio with mum. 'I took Brooklyn to work with me as much as possible,' says Victoria. 'He was talking away as I recorded and it sounded so cute I left it on the record.'

This album is about laying the myths to rest. Victoria's deeply personal lyrics speak volumes about her outlook on life, love and family. But most impressive of all is the diversity of her musical talents. She shows herself as a sophisticated pop singer in her own right.

As Victoria herself says, 'I have spent eighteen months putting this album together – hopefully people will see that there is a bit more to Victoria Beckham than a pout and a trip down Bond Street!' **'Victoria Beckham'** is released by Virgin Records on 1st October 2001.

Victoria Beckham solo material
- Single: **'Not Such An Innocent Girl'**, release – 17 September
- Album: **'Victoria Beckham'**, release – 1 October
- Autobiography: **'Learning To Fly'**, release – 13 September
- Website: www.victoriabeckham.mu, launch 24 July

As part of the Spice Girls, Victoria has sold over 40 million albums and 25 million singles worldwide.

For more information contact: Gordon on 0208 968 9000
E-mail: gordon.apb@which.net

Produce a web page for the imaginary band you created in the previous activity.

For advice on how to design web pages, see pages 198–9.

Write an **evaluation** *of your web page, explaining your intentions and your chosen target market and identifying features which could be improved.*

For advice about writing evaluations, see page 51.

Produce a storyboard for the opening shots of a promotional video for an imaginary band.

The opening should show the band as a group and then focus on each individual. Design the **appearance** *of the band members and the* **settings** *in which they appear. Write notes to accompany your storyboard, explaining your decisions.*

Use a **variety of camera shots** *and movements and explain in your notes why you have selected them. Make up* **lyrics** *for the soundtrack.*

Write an **evaluation** *of any production you complete, stating clearly the aims of the production and to what extent these were achieved.*

For advice about writing evaluations, see page 51.

Exam practice ▬▬▬▬▬▬▬▬

Record the openings (about three minutes each) of three different styles of television music programmes. Watch these three or four times, making notes after the second, third and fourth viewing.

1   How are these clips typical of television pop music programmes?

2   Choose one clip. State one way it resembles the other clips and one way in which it is different.

3   How do the presenters talk to the television audience?
    How do their styles differ? What kind of audience are they trying to communicate with?

4   **a**   Make up a title for a new television music programme aimed at teenagers.
    b   Devise a running order (list of music) for one programme.
    c   List the features of the programme that will appeal to teenagers.
    d   Explain how the features will attract a teenage audience.

Advertising

>> *This chapter covers:*

* analysing print and moving image advertisements
* ethical aspects of advertising
* different types of advertising
* why advertising is necessary
* advertising and the media
* how advertisers can use shock tactics
* how advertising can work by stealth
* advertising and ethnic minorities
* advertising and new technology
* how Pepsi Cola went blue
* the first TV advertisements
* how to plan an advertising campaign
* exam practice.

READING THE MEDIA | Advertisements

Advertisements are messages which are intended to influence or persuade the people who receive them. As the media in general attract large audiences, they are needed by the advertisers in order to spread those messages. The activities and case studies in this chapter will help you to understand that relationship.

Select one print advertisement and one television advertisement. Describe and analyse them with the help of the following questions and guidelines.

How can you distinguish an advertisement from the rest of the newspaper or magazine in which it appears?

How can you recognise the difference between a television advert and a television programme?

Look for and describe examples of these advertising conventions:

- a **brand name** and/or logo being emphasised
- a **contact** or **action line/statement** – that is, one urging you to act quickly, e.g. 'Buy now' or 'Sale ends tomorrow'
- **factual information**, e.g. 'New Jeep Grand Cherokee Overland – its 4.7 litre 255bhp V8 develops 11% more torque and 16% more horsepower than the standard V8'
- **verbal persuasion**, e.g. 'The Valencian region is full of good reasons for choosing this destination for your next holiday. Book today. Don't miss out'
- **selling points** – that is, the things that are special about the product/service, e.g. 'What makes the QEII so legendary? Things like five tea services every afternoon ... seven restaurants under the steady hands of fifty chefs'
- visual **images** which try to **impress**, **create desire or shock** – these can be found in non-advertising material, but in adverts the visual images are either of the product/service being advertised or are closely linked with them
- **slogans or catchphrases,** e.g. 'Probably the best lager in the world'
- **celebrities** recommending or being associated with a product, e.g. Tiger Woods endorsed Nike by making a commercial in which he performs tricks with a golf club and a ball.

Record a number of advertisements from television and describe and analyse them using the following instructions and guidelines.

- *Describe an example of a **character** whom the viewer is encouraged to identify with or to envy.*
- *Describe an example of a **playlet**, where either a problem is solved with the help of the product being advertised or a situation develops over time, as in the Nescafé Gold Blend adverts.*
- *Describe an example of a **documentary-style** sequence, i.e. an advertisement that shows **real-life** situations, as in the Department of Health's anti-smoking advertisement where, in two separate films, a 30-year-old man and his daughter talk about the effects of lung cancer. Describe an example of a **TV or film character** in advertising narratives. Explain why that particular character has been chosen. Describe an example of the use of an object which has acquired a particular meaning through being widely used in advertising.*

Advert for Rimmel lipstick

For example:

- *a Porsche car indicates wealth and power*
- *dogs suggest loyalty*
- *beer is linked with masculinity*
- *spectacles suggest cleverness*
- *well-filled bookshelves convey intelligence.*

▶ *Choose one example of the skilful use of **music** and/or **sound effects.** Explain why it is effective.*

▶ *Choose one example of an effective **voice-over** and say why the particular voice has been chosen. For example, a bright and enthusiastic voice may give the impression of excitement or friendliness. A more intimate, seductive voice can suggest sex appeal. Regional accents can suggest down-to-earth ordinariness or familiarity, while standard accents can be authoritative.*

▶ *Look out for editing techniques being used to associate two different objects or objects and people. For instance, a picture of a beautiful woman can be dissolved into a picture of a car, or a handsome Arab can become a bar of Turkish Delight, thereby creating an association between the two for the viewer.*

▶ *Describe an example of an advert which in your opinion **exploits** people's emotions or weaknesses, and explain why you think this is so. For example, advertising campaigns for mobile phones often try to make people feel self-conscious about not having the latest model, with slogans like 'Ashamed of your mobile?' or 'Life contains enough embarrassments without your mobile being one.'*

Advertising, commerce and values

There are commercial reasons for advertising. Producers of any commodity or service need to sell what they produce to stay in business, and advertising is one means of promoting awareness and encouraging sales. The purpose of advertising is to **let people know** about the commodity or service and to persuade them of the **benefits** of buying or using it. Equally, the advertising medium, whether a television channel or a publishing house, needs the revenue it receives from advertising in order to survive commercially.

While an advert is telling us about products, it is also **encouraging certain lifestyles.**

Advertising can **create desires** that did not previously exist. This in turn may make people dissatisfied with their lives – particularly if they cannot afford the products which the advertiser is suggesting they need in order to be happy and successful.

Many adverts emphasise differences in products which are really very trivial. Some people argue that choices are made by the producers of goods rather than the consumers. When we are offered a choice between different washing-up liquids, for instance, the actual differences between brands are negligible: the important decisions about the products have already been made by the manufacturers.

Analysis of a print advertisement for Sharp LCD television

On 10 November 2001 several colour supplements featured a full-page colour advertisement for a new brand of Sharp LCD television.

Branding
The Sharp **brand name** was emphasised at the bottom right of the advertisement. While the predominant colours in the ad were cool blues, in contrast there were two touches of red: the chair and the word 'SHARP'. Because of the contrast, the eye was drawn to these warm colours, hovering between the picture and the brand name.

The brand name also appeared in white in the picture and under the product name AQUOS. It appeared three times in the text paragraph. This **repetition** helped to fix the name in the reader's mind.

Some limited **product information** was given. Readers were told that the screen was only 6 cm deep, that there were three different screen sizes and that pictures were sharp and bright, even when viewed from an angle. The advertisement also featured a discreet **action line**, including an Internet address and Freephone number.

Product
The main 'selling' was done by the picture. The product itself was displayed as the focal point of the room, positioned on a sleek, modern curved glass stand. Two figures emerged from the curved wall of the room, stretching out their hands towards the screen. They were running and seemed to be in perfect

physical harmony. They were both happy. Their gaze was fixed on the screen. The implied message was that what these attractive and successful people want was desirable – and that the reader should desire it too.

There was a sense of magic about the figures emerging from the wall as if they were able to pass through physical barriers. Thus the product was linked with the supernatural, hinting at a sense of wonder. The phrase 'new dimension' was repeated, suggesting a science-fiction world where people could move through solid objects and highlighting the scientific miracle of displaying television pictures on a thin LCD screen.

Characters
The two **characters** shown in the ad were young, fit, smartly but casually dressed and attractive rather than glamorous. The impression given was of successful, well-off, middle-class people who move with the times but without being superficially 'trendy'. They looked happy, full of vitality – the opposite of 'couch potatoes'.

Setting
The setting was their home: sleek, modern and sparsely furnished, its contents expensive and tasteful. The main source of light was from the window at the far end of the room. The couple seemed to be moving from the dark into the light, coming to life as they stretched out towards the screen.

Reader identification
Readers of the magazine were invited to **identify** with this couple, who were youthful, confident, active, middle-class and white. This could be the target audience of the magazine – people in their 20s and 30s, who are in a relationship, who own their own home and have disposable income.

Not all readers would have been television addicts: some might have had concerns about the effects of too much television-viewing – and the advert may have been meant to reassure them. The television was not shown as something to be watched slavishly. There were no seats in front of the television screen. It was presented more as a desirable item of furniture than a piece of technology.

It seems that the advert was meant to **appeal to young people** in a steady relationship but with no children, who regard themselves as up-to-date and stylish. The text emphasised this with the words 'Exciting, stylish and desirable.'

The advertisement was trying to sell a luxury product. In reality people do not need this advanced form of technology, but in order for Sharp to sell its products, it has to **create desire** among customers or else make them dissatisfied with what they already have. This is an important part of how capitalism works.

Analysis of an advertising campaign: Walkers Crisps

A campaign is the whole process of advertising a product and can involve different sorts of advertising at different times and in different media.

The **purpose** of this campaign was to increase awareness of the Walkers brand and to increase sales of their crisps.

Market research showed that people who liked eating crisps said that 'irresistibility' was the main thing that attracted them. They also said that they saw crisps as part of everyday life and would not take kindly to a brand that took itself too seriously. Though crisps were popular with children, who were purchasers in their own right, adults also liked them.

'Nice guy' Gary Lineker in a scene from a Walkers Crisps advert

The creative brief

One of the first tasks of an advertising agency is to develop a **creative brief** for the product or service it aims to sell. In this case, the brief was as follows:

- The advertising had to appeal to a mass audience of adults and children.
- The main idea was that 'no one can resist Walkers crisps'.
- The values that would be emphasised were fun, unpretentiousness, informality, classlessness and sociability.

The campaign strategy

Leicester-based Walkers had previously used the footballer Gary Lineker in its advertising campaigns, emphasising his status as a 'local hero'. Since Lineker had gone on to achieve national fame, the campaign team wanted to get across the idea that 'Walkers crisps are so irresistible that they even make nice guys turn nasty.' Lineker fitted this role because he was 'nice', famous and down-to-earth.

Media buying

These were the possible choices of media that could have been used:

- television
- newspapers (national, regional, local, freesheets)
- magazines
- radio
- cinema
- leaflets
- bus sides
- posters
- billboards
- leaflets
- point-of-sale
- e-mail
- Internet
- mailshots.

It was decided to use TV advertising because it provided a mass audience. Five 60-second adverts were filmed featuring Gary Lineker in mini-narratives. These were screened between January 1995 and January 1996, as follows:

- 'Welcome Home', January 1995
- 'Nun', March
- 'Garymania', May
- 'Dial-a-Prize', September
- 'Salt 'n' Lineker', January 1996.

'Welcome Home' featured Lineker returning to Leicester as a hero figure. A young fan offers him a crisp and Lineker finds it so irresistible that he runs off with the packet, young boy in pursuit.

The advertisements attracted much publicity, with TV coverage even on *News at Ten* and *The Big Breakfast,* and press coverage in all the national newspapers. The tabloids even competed to be the first with 'What's Gary up to now?' stories.

Effects

The advertising agency which devised the campaign had to assess its effectiveness. Research showed that the 'awareness index' (people who recognised the name 'Walkers' and associated it with crisps) had risen from 6 to 15 (average being 10) among children and from 8 to 24 among adults.

Research involving interviews to find people's attitudes to the product confirmed the popularity of Lineker. Typical of the responses were:

- 'I'd been told about the advert before I saw it. Very funny.' *(22-year-old)*
- 'There's not many people who could appeal across the board like him.' *(mother)*
- 'He's an idol, but because Walkers are so good he pinches them.' *(mother)*
- 'He can steal my crisps any time.' *(13-year-old girl)*

The 'Welcome Home' advert increased sales by 6 million bags.

Advertising and the media

The mass media attract **large audiences**, which the advertising industry needs. For example, *The Sun* newspaper and *Coronation Street* can provide an audience/market of about 10 million readers/viewers. Other specialised publications or programmes can provide **niche markets**: smaller numbers of people who share a common interest. For example, the magazine *Webuser* carries numerous adverts for computer software.

Without money from advertising, much of the huge variety of modern media would not exist. Most radio and television stations, newspapers and magazines and cinemas derive part or all of their revenue from advertising. All independent radio and television companies would fold, and newspapers would become so expensive that they would be bought only by the few who could afford them.

Market research

Media organisations conduct **market research** into the buying habits of their readers. They then try to sell advertising space to manufacturers who make the goods their readers want.

The Daily Telegraph is a broadsheet newspaper which relies on advertising for about three-quarters of its revenue. The table opposite shows the kind of detailed information about its readers that *The Daily Telegraph* can give to potential advertisers.

Discuss in small groups, using the notes as talking points, whether advertising is a good or bad thing.

Advertising is **good** because:

▸ it encourages the sale of mass-produced goods and is therefore a stimulus to production
▸ it creates employment
▸ it is not brainwashing, because people can ignore the messages if they want to
▸ It provides information about products so that consumers can make an informed choice about what they want to buy
▸ it is strictly regulated and tries to be legal, decent, honest and truthful.

Advertising is **bad** because:

▸ it makes people want things they do not need
▸ it encourages people to neglect urgent human needs in favour of fads and luxuries
▸ it encourages people to be greedy and selfish
▸ it makes us wasteful by always wanting new products and discarding old ones which could still be useful
▸ it does not benefit society as a whole, but serves only to make powerful commercial organisations richer.

In 1997, a document published by the Catholic Church entitled Ethics in Advertising *argued that advertising:*

- ▸ *promotes lifestyles which people cannot afford*
- ▸ *encourages the use of cars, which pollute the atmosphere*
- ▸ *encourages people to envy the rich and successful*
- ▸ *encourages lust*
- ▸ *is offensive when it treats religion flippantly*
- ▸ *exploits and stereotypes women.*

	Readers' likes	Readers' dislikes
Magazines	*Tatler* *National Geographic* *Saga* *The Economist* *Harpers and Queen* *Private Eye*	TV listings magazines *Smash Hits* Motorbike mags *Woman's Realm*
TV programmes	Channel 4 News Gardeners' World Newsnight Golf	The Big Breakfast Coronation Street Stars in Their Eyes
Statements	'I read the financial pages of the papers' 'I try to take more than one holiday abroad each year' 'A woman's place is in the home'	'A real man can down several pints at one sitting' 'I only work for the money' 'I look forward to more TV channels'
Cheese	Brie Stilton Camembert	Cottage cheese Cheshire Caerphilly
Breakfast cereals	Alpen Common Sense Fruit and Fibre Sultana Bran	Pop Tarts Cheerios Banana Bubbles
Cars	Jaguar Mercedes Audi	Ford Vauxhall Lada

Advertising and publicity

Advertisers need to **attract publicity for their products**. Advertising space has to be purchased, but publicity costs nothing. Advertising agencies can employ **PR (public relations)** companies who specialise in headline-grabbing stunts. For example:

- The 'pregnant man' campaign for the Health Education Council in the 1970s attracted more press coverage than advertising space.
- Coca-Cola deliberately used a black model for its first Fanta advertisement in order to be able to run the press story, 'Coca-Cola uses first black model in its advertising campaigns.'

Sometimes, advertisers also deliberately run **controversial adverts** which are banned and thus generate huge amounts of free coverage in the media. Benetton is noted for this, as are Club 18–30 and Tango.

Sometimes, advertising agencies will even secure publicity just by offering a part in an ad to someone famous. Cadbury, the makers of Milk Tray, once released a statement implying that they had invited Robbie Williams to star in their new advertisement: 'The UK's leading heart-throb, Robbie, is the ideal candidate to take on the task of starring in the new ads.' Robbie Williams' record company issued a denial, but the free publicity had already been achieved.

The three big selling points for getting press coverage – particularly in the tabloids – are **sex**, **controversy** and **celebrities**. There is an old saying in advertising that if you haven't got an idea, get a celebrity. The creator of the Gary Lineker campaign *(see above)* is quoted as saying:

> 'PR should never be the main reason for using a celebrity, but I'd be lying if I said it didn't help. It can get you fantastic amounts of free publicity. When we put Anna Kournikova on a poster for Berlei sports bras the campaign cost around £500,000 but the media coverage we got was worth several million.'

However, celebrities can be **counter-productive** if they suddenly become unpopular. For example, Pepsi lost out when Michael Jackson became involved in child abuse allegations and Mike Tyson was reported to have punched his wife.

Shock tactics in advertising

Sometimes, advertisers use **shock tactics**. This can be effective but it can also risk alienating the target audience. Shock tactics which go too far can be banned by the **Advertising Standards Authority (ASA)**.

There were complaints in 1995 when an insurance company, Sun Alliance, showed situations which depicted the world as a dangerous place – babies next to boiling water, a church cross falling on a car, a child with a gun and so on. The ASA did not ban the adverts, but did report that some viewers felt that their emotions were being exploited. Rule 16 of the Independent Television Commission's rules on advertising states:

> 'Advertisements must not without justifiable reason play on fear.'

One 'justifiable reason' is put forward by **charities**, who argue that people are becoming immune to their appeals and need to be shocked into action. The adverts must not, however, shock to the extent that people feel despair or hopelessness.

The RSPCA used an image of dead dogs with the message: 'It doesn't take long to turn a Jock or Spot or Sandy into a small pile of ashes.' It was used in a campaign arguing that abolishing the licence system would lead to an increase in the number of abandoned dogs.

The Campaign for Racial Equality deliberately used racist stereotypes in a campaign that showed a white woman looking nervously at a black man on a bus above the words: 'It's a jungle out there.' A few days later, follow-up ads asked the question: 'What was worse? This ad or your failure to complain about it?' The ASA ruled that this tactic was 'irresponsible'.

The changing face of advertising

Advertising is moving on because of **changing technology**. TV advertising is moving away from its norm of 'interruptive' 60-second ads. The development of set-top boxes by **TiVo** and **Replay**, which allow viewers to compile their own schedules and 'zap out' any commercials, will lead to smaller audiences.

There is an increasing trend towards advertisers **sponsoring** programmes rather than simply paying to advertise in commercial breaks. In the USA, the programmes themselves contain the brands – a method known as **product placement**. Advertisers may also **make their own programmes.**

One important phenomenon is the rise of **interactive advertising.** A viewer who has a digital television with a set-top box is able to respond to an on-screen message which indicates when an advert is interactive. When a remote-control button is pressed, the conventional advert shrinks and the rest of the screen displays recipes, orders for money-off vouchers, competitions, quizzes – anything to make the viewer focus on the product the advertiser wants to sell. The advertiser thus holds the viewer's attention for several minutes rather than a mere 30 seconds.

The first interactive television advert was in March 2000, for Chicken Tonight. It was 70% more successful than an ordinary TV commercial.

Advertising by stealth

Some advertisers use **stealth advertising** – that is, advertising without the viewer being aware of it. Playstation 2 was advertised by sequences that did not seem to be advertising anything. One showed a weird image of a hyper-wrinkled old woman above the line:

'I am horse, sinew, muscle and hoof. I am thunder across your land.'

The thinking behind the campaign was that the audience was becoming jaded with conventional adverts. The manufacturers of Playstation wanted to position themselves as a cutting-edge, alternative games provider. The campaign was aimed at intriguing people and making them wonder what was going on. Once word got round, the people who were in the know felt 'special' and superior.

Another example was in the film *Top Gun*, which was partly sponsored by the American Air Force and the makers of sunglasses. The recruits in the film wore sunglasses much of the time, and the result was a glut of eager Air Force recruits and an unprecedented rise in the sale of sunglasses.

Advertising and ethnic minorities

The last years of the twentieth century saw a significant increase in the representation of ethnic minorities in British commercials. This was partly as a result of increases in the proportion of blacks and Asians in the UK, and partly because the spending power of certain groups was increasing. The London Research Centre in 1997 found that Indians, Chinese and African Asians (e.g. Ugandans) had higher average incomes per household than white people.

Although Caribbeans had lower average incomes, young black Brits were seen as important by advertisers because they were regarded as style gurus and leaders of fashion. Hence the predominance of black faces in advertisements for US clothing companies like Gap, Levi's, Diesel and DKNY. There has also been an increase in the use of blacks and Asians in adverts promoting everyday products such as washing powder or washing-up liquids, Oxo, and ads for well-known organisations such as the National Savings Bank and the Halifax Building Society. Previously, blacks in advertising had been mainly celebrities such as Lenny Henry or sports stars selling sports equipment.

Advertising and the Internet

Advertising on the Internet is increasing rapidly. In 1994, the Internet was virtually an advertisement-free zone. By 1996, Yahoo had over 50,000 companies advertising on its sites. In 2000, a new Nissan car was launched in the USA by the advertising agency sending out 12 students on a coast-to-coast drive with digital camcorders linked to the Web.

Advertising on the Internet ranges from simple information about a company and its products to lavish promotions like those for Pepsi or Levi's, which are rich in trickery and more like lifestyle magazines than simple advertising. Advertisers attract viewers by having interactive banners on websites. These are advertising strips along the side of a site, which when clicked lead you into the advertiser's own website.

Advertisers are realising that the Web is different from other advertising media. You have to make a deliberate decision to visit a site. With a product like Levi's, there is only so much information you can give, so you have to restrict the message to something that people actually want to read, see or hear.

Location-based advertising is possible on the Internet. This allows advertisers to direct their message to a specific locality, based on postcodes. For instance, Pizza Hut can send online pizza ads from local restaurants to nearby office workers when they are thinking about buying lunch. Chrysler car dealers in Holland have started sending Web ads only to people in their vicinity.

Guinness came up with the idea of using one of its television ads as a **screensaver** which could be downloaded. The result was that in offices all over the country Guinness advertising was being shown on computer screens – all at no cost to the company.

The first TV adverts

Britain's first-ever TV commercial was a 60-second slot advertising **Gibbs SR toothpaste**. It was transmitted at 8.12pm on 22 September 1955 on ITV during a variety programme called *Channel Nine*.

It featured a tube of toothpaste, a block of ice and a commentary about its 'tingling fresh' qualities. It was in fact an adaptation of a press advert and according to its creator was 'a bit like an illustrated lecture'. In fact, many early commercials had too many words (the result of the influence of radio) and too many long shots (the influence of cinema).

Like the advert for Gibbs SR, many early TV commercials were **adapted from printed adverts**. Crosse & Blackwell's started with a picture of its press advert which 'came to life' as the camera moved in. Persil ads were based on cartoon treatments of their posters, with dancers and sailors in different shades of white.

Advertisers paid to advertise in **time spots**, which showed the television station's clock so that viewers could set their own clocks and watches. Products such as Ever-rite watches, Saxa Salt and Aspro were advertised in these spots, as were some cigarettes: 'Time to light a Red and White. Just the job for a man who inhales'. These time slots with their advertising were thought to be annoying, and they were discontinued in December 1960.

Another early form of television advertising was the **admag**. This was like a soap opera setting with dialogue that had a story of sorts, but basically mentioned lots of products that advertisers were paying to have included in the script.

An example of this was *Jim's Inn*, which first appeared in 1957 and ran until 1963. It was set in a pub in a fictitious village called Wembleham. It had realistic storylines, a friendly pub landlord and characters with whom viewers could identify.

Changing image: Pepsi goes blue

Does colour matter? Pepsi Cola thought so. When it found that it was losing its share of the market to its rival Coca-Cola, it decided that this was because it didn't look different. So it spent $200 million on re-designing and advertising its cans in 'Project Blue'.

Pepsi Cola directors had seen the success of McDonald's red and yellow colour scheme. The colours actually stimulate the appetite, but by not allowing you to relax, they also encourage you to move on – the perfect formula for fast-food restaurants.

Pepsi Cola directors thought that blue looked cool and refreshing and that it suggested reliability and traditional values. So they went for the re-design.

Did it work? Pepsi's sales in the UK after the launch of the new can in 1996 went down by 12%, but the company argued that that was partly due to a poor summer.

READING THE MEDIA

Gender portrayal in advertisements

From the advertisements you study, collect or describe examples of the ways in which men and women are portrayed.

In particular, look for images of men being/appearing:

▶ silly
▶ desirable
▶ victimised

▶ powerful
▶ caring
▶ sexually desirable.

Look also for images of men:

▶ doing housework
▶ doing DIY
▶ engaged in sport.

Look for examples of women being/appearing:

▶ caring
▶ in control
▶ in authority

▶ victimised
▶ desirable
▶ fit/healthy.

Look also for images of women:

▶ doing housework
▶ doing DIY
▶ engaged in sport.

Use your findings to draw conclusions about how men and women are depicted in advertising. Present your conclusions as a talk or display.

MAKING THE MEDIA

Plan an advertising campaign

Your task is to devise an advertising campaign for a new fragrance. The selling points of the fragrance are:

▶ it makes people more attractive to the opposite sex
▶ it has a subtle and sophisticated odour which lasts for 24 hours
   it is made from pure ingredients
   it makes your skin more radiant.

*Decide on your **target market**. The cost of the fragrance will determine which people will be able to afford to buy it.*
*Assess the **competition**. Look at adverts for other fragrances and work out*

how yours can be different.

*Decide what **media** you will use for your campaign. Remember that although television appeals to mass audiences it is also the most expensive medium to use. It is advisable to use at least **two types** of media. Choose from:*

▶ *television (state which programmes would attract the right audience for your product, e.g. if you are aiming at a youthful audience, you could advertise during a popular soap opera like Hollyoaks)*

▶ *newspapers (national, regional, local)*

▶ *magazines (define which type, e.g. women's, lads, teenage girls, etc.)*

▶ *radio (state which types of programme on which radio stations, e.g. early morning pop music on Kiss FM)*

▶ *billboards (decide on location, e.g. near colleges, near nightclubs).*

*You could decide to employ a famous **celebrity** to endorse your fragrance and perhaps base your television advert on him/her.*

Spread your campaign out over six weeks. Decide when people are most likely to buy fragrance – in the summer, at Christmas?

*Prepare some **sample advertising** materials to show the maker of the fragrance what your advertising will look like. For example:*

▶ *a storyboard of about 15–20 frames for a 30-second TV advert*

▶ *a sketch of a full-page magazine advert*

▶ *a script for a 30-second radio advert*

▶ *a sketch for a billboard poster.*

*Write an **evaluation** of your campaign, in which you describe the research you made into your target market and into other advertising.*

Which parts of your campaign might benefit from some changes or revisions?

For advice about writing evaluations, see page 51.

Produce an advertisement.

Turn one of your sample adverts (for print, radio or television) into a final production.

Write an evaluation to cover your intentions and the effectiveness of your advert.

Exam practice ▬▬▬▬▬▬

Record two 30-second television adverts for different versions of the same sort of products, e.g. two different car adverts or two different household products. They should contain images of both men and women.

Watch these adverts three or four times, taking notes each time apart from the first viewing, then answer these questions:

1   How can you tell that you are watching adverts rather than television programmes? Give your reasons.
2   What kind of audience are the advertisements aimed at? Give reasons.
3   Explain how the adverts are trying to influence the audience.
4   Discuss the representation of gender in the two adverts.
5   List three camera shots used in the extracts. Briefly explain why they have been used.
6   a   Write a creative brief (see page 166) for a 30-second commercial which advertises a similar type of product to one of those you have been watching.
    b   Invent a name for your product and state three reasons why people should buy it.
    c   Explain which channel(s) you would show your adverts on and during which programmes. Give your reasons.
    d   Draw the first few frames of a storyboard for the advert you have described in question 2, identifying key shots and soundtrack.

Radio

>> *This chapter covers:*

- analysing local radio
- the roles of radio presenters
- different types of radio audience
- stereotyping of daytime audiences
- representation of popular music
- how to analyse radio news programmes
- voice quality
- producing a radio magazine programme
- exam practice on news selection and presentation.

READING THE MEDIA

Analysing radio

Logos for Heart fm radio and Severn Sound

In their *Radio Handbook*, Peter Wilby and Andrew Coroy write:

> Radio is an intimate medium. These days *[1993]* people rarely sit round the kitchen table in groups listening to the radio. It addresses each listener as an individual. When a radio is playing to a group of people, it is often to function as background sound in a place of work activity where listeners are able to entertain their private thoughts, their silent dialogue with the presenter or their personal associations with each record played while performing their routine tasks.

The activities below are designed to help you do your own analyses to see if this is still true today.

Compare and contrast local and national radio, using the directions and guidelines below.

Record and listen to local and national versions of the same type (genre) of programme. For instance:

- *a sports report on Five Live and one from your local commercial station*
- *a Radio 4 news broadcast and one from your local BBC station*
- *a breakfast record programme from Radio 1 and one from your local commercial station*
- *a late-night chat show from talkSPORT and any local radio station.*

*Describe how the programme **presenters** differ in terms of accents, delivery styles and attitudes. In what ways are they similar?*

*Compare **references** and **locations** in terms of whether they are local or national. For instance, national programmes might refer to the Scottish Highlands as 'remote', but for someone listening to Radio Stornoway, London is 'remote'. Local radio tends to have biased commentaries, favouring local teams, whereas national radio must aim to be non-partisan.*

*Compare the **sorts of information** given out in news broadcasts. Make notes on examples of items which would be irrelevant to a national audience, but important to a local one.*

Describe and analyse the role of a local radio presenter.

State which of these roles the presenter plays and quote examples:

- *entertainer*
- *counsellor or friend*
- *the man or woman in the street*
- *permanent public relations person*
- *DJ*
- *interviewer*
- *source of constant good humour*
- *cross between a showbusiness personality and a journalist.*

*Does the presenter impose his or her **values** and **attitudes** on the listener, whether in relation to music, politics or sport, or does he/she try to reflect the typical listener's values, to be the moderate 'voice of common sense'?*

*Describe the presenter's **voice quality**. Does he/she have a regional accent? Is the voice deep or high, is it relaxing or stimulating?*
*Describe the presenter's **style of talk**. Is it quick-fire or slow pace, urgent or casual? Some presenters try to be informal, friendly and matey, others try to speak with authority. Some may flirt with other presenters or with the listener.*

*Note the **kinds of questions** that the presenter asks. Are they the kind that most listeners would want to ask? How far does the presenter use **e-mails** and **text messages** to encourage listener involvement?*

Investigate the way in which radio stations match programmes with audiences.

Note: You will need to listen to programmes from different stations and at different times to be able to answer these questions.

*Describe examples of how different **sorts of programmes** are broadcast at different times of the day. Look for examples of the following pattern of programming:*

▶ *pre-working day*
▶ *daytime*
▶ *drive time*
▶ *evening.*

Describe how programme content changes to suit different times. For instance, breakfast radio has a format of short interviews, morning paper reviews, frequent time-checks and brief news bulletins.

*Describe what **different types of audiences** there will be at different times of the day and what those audiences might want from a radio programme. Conduct some research among friends and family to find out who listens to what at different times.*

*Listen to examples of **evening music programmes** which aim at **specialist audiences.** Describe one programme briefly, saying what sort of audience you think it has.*

▶ *How far is it still true that specialist programmes have presenters and audiences who like to think they are different from the masses who buy Top 40 records?*
▶ *Are records by indie bands thought to be superior to those produced by mainstream companies?*
▶ *Is rock seen not just as something that happens while you are having fun, but something which has to be valued for itself? Express your opinions and give evidence to support them.*

Radio audiences

In the **pre-working-day slot**, there is a wide-ranging audience with an equal balance of men and women, covering all age groups from schoolchildren to pensioners. At this time of day, listeners like programmes that help them wake up, give them snippets of information and sound cheerful. The audience is mostly on the move, with very few people listening for more than half an hour at a stretch.

Radio 1's image of its **evening audience** in 1989 was described as:

> 'school or college students doing their homework or staying in because they have no money to go out.'

The producers believed that, because young people had no money to buy records by fairly obscure bands, it was the duty of the station to 'provide that missing musical education for them'.

In **drive time** programmes, the music is less urgent and more relaxing than in the morning programmes, helping the listener to unwind after a hard day's work. The tone of the presenters is also different: they are trying to calm people down rather than wake them up.

Programmes broadcast during the **daytime** (i.e. between 9 am and 4 pm) are often aimed at a female audience. Here are some examples of how radio stations and radio presenters imagined their **female listeners:**

> 'There are certain fundamentals that women enjoy. Women are sentimental, or they care deeply about emotions... They are escapists, or they are not sufficiently cold-blooded to enjoy drama.'
>
> Capital Radio, 1973

Radio 1 in its early days believed that during the day it was broadcasting to an audience of housewives, typically:

> '... a figure who I think of as someone who two years ago was a secretary working for a firm, who is now married and has a child. She wants music that will keep her happy and on the move.'
>
> Derek Chinnery, radio producer (1977)

In the same year, Radio 1 DJ David Hamilton said that he imagined his typical listener to be:

> '... a housewife, young at heart, probably on her own virtually every day. She's bored with the routine of housework and with her own company and for her I'm the slightly cheeky romantic visitor.'

This is from a radio producer in 1986:

> 'We call our average listener Doreen. She isn't stupid, but she's only listening with half an ear, and doesn't necessarily understand "long words". This doesn't mean that we treat her like a fool but that we make sure that she understands first time, because when listening to radio you can't re-read what's just been said as you can in a newspaper.'

There was a move in the late 80s, on Steve Wright's afternoon show in particular, to recognise that 'liberated' women had sexual lives and liked sexual banter. But the tone of daytime music radio still reflected an assumption that women were basically home-loving and obsessed with romance.

This assumption was also reflected in the choice of music, which could be said to remind women at home of the way they were before they were married and had children. Typical songs were about a first kiss, a summer romance or a blind date, or else reminded women of their past, when they went to parties.

Investigate the role of advertising in radio.

Record two commercial radio programmes aimed at different audiences. You could compare a daytime programme aimed at 'main shoppers' with a specialist evening programme aimed at under-25s.

Try to work out the connection between the type of audience a programme attracts and the products and services which are being advertised.
Make a chart to show your findings, with a list of adverts and a description of the respective audiences.
It is worth trying to obtain information about composition of audiences from the radio station's advertising or marketing department.

Compare the way popular music is represented on two contrasting music programmes.

Record two different sorts of music programme and use the following questions to help you to compare them.

*What sort of **audience** is the selection likely to appeal to?*
For example:

▸ *people going to work*
▸ *housewives at home during the day*
▸ *specialist audiences during the evening.*

*What sort of **DJ** is there?*

▸ *Is the DJ male or female? What age is he/she?*
▸ *What **sort of music** does the DJ play? Is it chart music or indie? Is it specialist or general? Is the emphasis on variety, or is it all one kind of music?*
▸ *Find out what sort of musical **likes and dislikes** the DJ has. The DJ probably does not pick the records, though some do. You can tell the DJ's opinions about some particular tracks or artists by noting statements like this:*

> *'So Westlife's video is showing them doing things you didn't know they did. Like playing musical instruments and composing their own songs, I suppose.'*

▸ *Is the DJ **alone** or with a partner or groups of people? Some DJs will try to make it sound as if they are talking directly to the listener like a close friend. Others try to have a lot of banter going on with people in the studio to create a feeling of being out with a group of lively friends.*
▸ *How does the DJ **address** the audience? Is there a style of rapid-fire delivery? This came from America and accompanied rock and roll. It came to Britain via pirate radio and a mid-Atlantic accent (a mixture of English and American) became fashionable.*
▸ *Does the DJ think that he/she is a **star** or a **servant,** a show-off or a helper?*

Present your conclusions in a short radio package, with comments of your own and brief extracts from the music programmes you have studied.

Radio presenter and DJ Neil Fox

Describe two different types of radio news programmes.

For example:

▸ brief **headline**-type snippets, which are broadcast from time to time on music programmes

▸ **half-hour bulletins** on Radio 4 at 6pm and midnight.

What **type of story** is included and which stories are given prominence?

▸ News programmes are sometimes labelled, using newspaper terminology, as 'broadsheet' news or 'tabloid'. **Broadsheet** news deals seriously with politics and social events at home and abroad. Its delivery requires the presenter to have a very good knowledge of current affairs. **Tabloid** news centres around human interest stories, sport, showbiz and celebrity gossip, and its delivery is often by funny, zany presenters.

What **different techniques** are used to present the news? For example:

▸ **copy news** is read out from a script, which is written either by the newsreader or a broadcast journalist

▸ **packages** are pre-recorded and are introduced by a reporter speaking directly to the listener

▸ **newsclips** are extracts from press conferences, which are recorded on cartridges which are then played by the newsreader

▸ **live reports** are made from radio cars, which act like mobile studios and can be taken to the source of the story

▸ **live broadcasts** from press conferences or parliament are included in some magazine programmes such as Radio Five Live in the afternoon. Live broadcasts give the listener a feeling of being present as news is being made, but they are also unpredictable and difficult to schedule. Such items are sometimes summarised or commented on immediately by special correspondents or experts in the studio.

What **style of delivery** does the newsreader have?

▸ Quality of voice is important for creating the right kind of atmosphere and image in a news broadcast. Some newsreaders such as Brian Perkins or Charlotte Green of Radio 4 sound serious and dignified. They pronounce words very clearly and they do not have regional accents. Others have a more relaxed style of delivery and maybe a regional accent to create a different impression, perhaps one of friendliness.

Radio voices

Sally Boazman

Nicky Campbell

Natalie Wheen

John Peel

These are descriptions of presenters' and newsreaders' voices taken from a Radio Times poll for 'the most attractive voice on radio':

* **Sally Boazman**
  Sally Travel, *Radio 2*
  'Boazman's warm tones and saucy chuckle are the only known antidotes to road rage.'

* **Fi Glover**
  Presenter, *Radio 5 Live*
  'Semi-flippant tone mixed with hint of the husky makes Glover perfect late-night listening.'

* **Natalie Wheen**
  Presenter, *Classic FM*
  'A voice as warm as toast.'

* **Nicky Campbell**
  Presenter, *Radio 5 Live*
  'Campbell's voice has the right mix of seriousness and accessibility for news debates.'

* **Henry Kelly**
  Presenter, *Classic FM*
  'Genial Irishman with a conversational style that really does come naturally.'

* **John Peel**
  Presenter, *Radio 1 and Radio 4*
  'Peel breathes reassurance into every syllable. One of radio's most comforting voices.'

* **Terry Wogan**
  Presenter, *Radio 2*
  'Masterful command of beautifully modulated practised informality.'

Produce a package for a radio magazine programme.

A package:

▸ *usually lasts between 2–5 minutes*
▸ *has a reporter introducing either informal chats or formal interviews*
▸ *normally follows the pattern of describing a general situation, then giving some examples to illustrate it, finishing off with a general summing up.*

*Define your **target audience**. How old? What gender? Where are they? What are their interests?*

*Choose a **topic** to report on. For example:*

▸ *current news stories about teenagers*
▸ *new developments where you live*
▸ *young workers being exploited*
▸ *bad/good effects of television*
▸ *nostalgia (the way things used to be)*
▸ *reviews of new films or programmes*
▸ *fashion changes.*

*Conduct **research** into the topic. This might involve reading, but is more likely to involve talking to people with specialist knowledge.*

***Select** people to interview. Contact them and arrange times and venues. Choose your locations carefully. It is good to have some background noise for some topics, but don't overdo it.*

*Conduct **interviews**.*

***Edit** interviews and write a script for your introductions and links. Try splitting the interviews up into separate parts with a presenter's words linking them.*

***Record** your scripted words.*

*Edit your material, **adding music** where appropriate.*

*Write an **evaluation** of your package, using the following questions:*

▸ *How did you decide on your target audience?*
  What research did you do and what problems did you encounter?
  How did you cope with the problem of timing your package precisely?
  What editing challenges did you have and how did you overcome them?
  How did a sample audience react to your package?
  How would you improve your work?

For advice about writing evaluations, see page 51.

Exam practice ▪▪▪▪▪▪▪▪▪▪▪▪▪▪▪▪

1   You have applied for a job as the news editor on a new local radio station. The station wants to attract young listeners. You have been asked to make proposals for a new style of news programme which would appeal to the 16–18 age range.

   a   What kinds of news stories would you plan to include?

   b   What sort of presenter/s would you hire?

   c   What sort of introductory music/sound effects would you have?

2   From the following news stories, compile a 5-minute news broadcast aimed at a family audience during the breakfast slot.

   a   Decide which stories you would include and which material.

   b   Decide on a running order and give reasons for your choices.

   c   Write a script for the opening of the programme and the first story.

Local girl's success on 'Pop Idol'

17-year-old Lisa Soulsby has won through to the last 16 of the current *Pop Idol* TV show. The programme has a national audience of over 10 million. Though some of the judges were quite rude about Lisa's 'karaoke-style' delivery of 'Secret Love', the viewers at home voted for her in their millions.

Material available:

- 20-second interview with Lisa
- 15-second extract from the TV performance of the song
- 20 seconds of rude comments by one of the judges
- 20-second interview with Lisa's mum.

A duck that will only eat Chinese takeaways

A duck at a local wildfowl centre was off its food until one of the workers left the remains of her Chinese takeaway near its pond. The duck gobbled the left-overs up in seconds. The staff have discovered that the way to restore the duck's appetite is to mix normal duck food like maggots with fried rice.

Material available:

- 30-second interview with a worker from the wildfowl centre
- 20-second interview with a representative of the Royal Society for the Protection of Birds.

School trip disaster

One pupil was killed and 30 injured, some seriously, when a coach carrying pupils from a local school overturned on a motorway slip road in France. The reason for the crash, which happened in the early hours of this morning, has not been established. There is an emergency number for parents and friends to ring for more information.

Material available:

- live link with French police
- live link with reporter at school
- recorded 30-second description of scene by a French journalist.

Local soccer club sacks manager

The local Premiership soccer team has just sacked its manager. The sacking comes as a big shock as he had been quite successful. There are several rumours about a rift between the club chairman and the manager. One possible reason is that the chairman wants to sell a star player because the club have been offered over £30 million for him but the manager wants to keep him.

Material available:

- 20-second interview with supporters' club spokesperson
- 30-second 'vox pop' with some fans
- live interview with the radio station's sports editor.

Local farm blamed for Foot and Mouth crisis

A local farmer has been found guilty of causing the Foot and Mouth epidemic which devastated the nation's farming industry. Billy Wardle was found to have fed his pigs on infected slops which were collected from local schools. The food was not processed properly before being given to the animals. Mr Wardle failed to recognise the symptoms of the disease in his animals and sent them to different slaughterhouses around the country, thereby causing the biggest Foot and Mouth epidemic in history. Mr Wardle will be sentenced tomorrow.

Material available:

- 20-second interview with Billy's brother
- 20-second interview with representative of the Farmers' Union
- 30-second report from a reporter who attended the court case.

Gran finds earrings in trifle

Edna Skinner was shocked when she found a pair of earrings in a trifle she had just bought from a local supermarket. She said they could have done some real damage if she had swallowed them.

Material available:

- 15-second interview with Edna
- 20-second interview with the manager of the supermarket
- 10-second interview with local jeweller.

New hostel for refugees

A new hostel to help cater for the growing numbers of refugees seeking asylum in the UK is to be created in the area. It will house up to 300 families. A derelict former mental hospital will be converted at a cost of £3 million. Local residents' groups are opposed to the scheme, but the local MP is in favour.

Material available:

- 30-second interview with spokesperson for asylum-seekers
- 20-second interview with local MP
- 20-second interview with representative of local residents group.

Woman mugged in park

A 65-year-old woman was attacked and robbed yesterday as she walked home from the shopping centre through a park. She was stopped by three youths, who threatened her and ran off with her handbag. The woman had just been to collect her pension. Police say that there has been a spate of such attacks recently. They have issued a description of the youths involved.

Material available:

- 20-second interview with police spokesperson
- 20-second interview with the woman attacked
- 30-second interview with a youth worker who has ideas on how to prevent such crimes.

Airliner on fire to make emergency landing

News is just coming in that an airliner carrying 300 passengers has reported a fire on board. The plane is trying to make an emergency landing at a local airfield.

Material available: none at the moment.

Hens lay hard-boiled eggs

A local farmer claims that he has produced hens which lay hard-boiled eggs. Arthur Nebulus, 45, says he has a secret feeding formula which increases the temperature of the hens' internal organs so that when the eggs are laid they are already cooked.

Material available:

- 2-minute interview with Arthur Nebulus.

Chapter 15

New technologies

>> *This chapter covers:*
- information about current media technology
- finding information about developments
  in media technology
- how to analyse computer games
- how to design your own website
- exam practice.

READING THE MEDIA

Media technology

The aim of this chapter is to give you some basic information about media technology current at the time of writing. You should read this first, then complete the activity which follows, concerning contemporary developments in the world of the media.

Terrestrial (land-based) television
The television channels BBC1, BBC2, ITV 1, Channel 4 and Five all depend on a network of transmitters which pass on UHF (Ultra High Frequency) signals from one to the other. The problem with this system is that expensive TV aerials are needed in hilly country where the signal is likely to be weak. An advantage is that regional programmes can be broadcast selectively to a single region and not to the rest of the national network.

Cable television
Cable television is transmitted through a network of underground cables. You do not need an aerial to receive the signals. However, you do need a decoder box to 'interpret' the signal.

Cable offers a wider choice of programmes than terrestrial TV. It can also be linked to a telephone system. People can only link to the network if cables have been laid in their area, and laying cables is expensive, time-consuming and disruptive. Viewers have to pay the cable company a fixed monthly fee depending on which channels they receive.

Digital television

Digital TV has a different way of transmitting signals. The signals are more concentrated and more compressed than the conventional analogue signals. This has three benefits:

- The pictures are clearer and sharper.
- Viewers have more control over the pictures on their screens, being able to zoom in on details or choose a camera angle, for example during coverage of sporting events.
- Many more programmes can be transmitted. This is important for the terrestrial channels because they can compete in terms of programme choice with satellite and cable operators.

Interactive television

This allows people to have access to home banking and shopping services that are not linked to television schedules. Viewers have remote-control boxes which allow them to deliver messages to television via telephone lines.

Pay-per-view

Viewers pay an additional fee to watch specific programmes, especially sports events. When BSkyB used this system in 1996, it earned £5 million by screening the fight between Mike Tyson and Frank Bruno.

Satellite

Signals are transmitted via satellites which orbit the earth. They are like space relay stations that can transmit from and to stations on the ground. Before the signals are transmitted to the satellite they are encoded. Viewers need satellite dishes on their houses to receive the signals and a decoding box to translate the signals. The signal will have travelled almost 50,000 miles, but the journey will have taken a quarter of a second. The commercial success of satellite television in the UK has depended on BSkyB securing rights to broadcast major sporting events.

Convergence

Increasingly, media companies control different parts of the communications process from production to distribution and reception. In the home, the movement is towards a central system from which all media products can be operated. Each home will be able to have a network of television screens, computers, phones and radios all linked with one central source.

Videophones

These were used in the reporting of American attacks on Afghanistan in 2001. They were particularly useful because the country had poor communications. Videophones allowed reporters to get into remote and hostile places and still transmit their reports live. Journalists simply had to unfold the satellite antenna, open the videophone box, connect the camera and transmit.

READING THE MEDIA

Compile information during your media studies course about any changes in the technology used by the media.

This is a long-term exercise which is best done as a co-operative class activity with an ongoing pooling of information. You will find information in the media sections of newspapers and on the Internet, especially in the media section of Guardian Unlimited: www.mediaguardian.co.uk.

▸ *Keep a file of notes and cuttings which describe significant technological advances in the media.*

▸ *Describe the media technology in your own home, how it is used and how it changes.*

Investigate the audience responses to changing technology.

The media industry depends on technology and is constantly changing in response to technological advances. For historical examples, you could consider the effect of the introduction of sound on the film industry or the effect of the advent of television on both radio and cinema.

*As far as contemporary media studies are concerned, you need not only to keep up to date with technological developments, but also to be aware of **how the audience reacts** to the changes and potential changes.*

▸ *Interview people from a variety of age groups and ask them about their feelings and thoughts concerning **digital broadcasting**.*

▸ *Note whether or not they have digital equipment. In particular, find out if they want the vast choice of TV programmes that digital technology offers.*

▸ *Interview people about whether they are aware of **broadband technology** and, if so, whether they want it. Broadband cables can make your connection to the Internet ten times faster, but phone-based systems are a hundred times faster. At these speeds, phone lines are capable of delivering good-quality video for video conferencing, movies and television. Video on demand is possible, but do people really want to watch films on their computers?*

Digital television

The replacement of the existing analogue system of transmitting television pictures with a digital system raises important questions. In 2001, only 25% of households had digital sets. By 2006, 65% are expected to have digital TV. But this will still leave 35% of households which do not want digital services.

Such households do not want more channels, or do not understand terms such as 'interactive', do not use e-mail or do not want to shop on television. As the government will earn several billion pounds in revenue from the sale of analogue frequencies to mobile telephone companies, it may have to encourage that reluctant 35% of households by supplying free digital conversion systems.

Journalist Polly Toynbee explains why people might be reluctant to invest in digital television:

> 'The trouble is that digital boxes and dishes have a downmarket, shell-suit image. Young, brash, vulgar, sports-pub, *Sun*-reading, Murdoch-tainted digital TV just does not have class.'

Internet recording

With the latest equipment it is now possible to produce a high-quality CD using a desktop PC or Mac. In 2001, Nick Cave recorded his album, *No More Shall We Part* on an Apple iMac. The hip-hop band The Method record all of their music on a PC because it saves paying the costs of a studio and sound engineer.

Digital desktop recording requires a modern computer with a minimum of 256MB of RAM and some music-making software such as Pro Tools or Cubase VST. A Musical Instrument Digital Input (Midi) keyboard and a good all-round microphone such as Shure SM58 are also very useful. Once the music is ready to be shared with an audience, it can be converted into an MP3 file using an MP3 encoder such as Media Box and posted on the Internet.

Websites which offer advice on Internet recording are:

- *www.peoplesound.com*
- *www.taxi.com*
- *www.rocketnetwork.com*
- *www.steinberg.net*
- *www.samplearena.com*
- *www.prosoniq.com*.

Audience options

One effect of new technology has been to **increase audience options.** For example, Internet news offers a great variety of choice for the consumer. There are several **mainstream news sites**:

- *BBC News Online, www.bbc.co.uk/news*
  This combines up-to-the-minute breaking news and background information. A flashing news update at the top of the screen draws attention to the latest developments, and a multimedia section contains selected audio and video clips. There are also clickable guides full of key

The home page of Reuters.com, the online service of the international news agency

facts, and a discussion room.

- *ITN, www.itn.co.uk*
  This has video clips and breaking news in its Virtual Newsroom. In the Channel 4 section the emphasis is on analysis.

- *Sky News, www.sky.com/news*
  This is one of the best sites for on-the-spot reports and the latest headlines.

- *Reuters, www.reuters.co.uk*
  A very good site for breaking news and pictures.

- *CNN Europe, http://europe.cnn.com*
  Quick, clear coverage of the latest events, with an 'In Depth' section for more detailed analysis.

- *Ananova, www.ananova.com*
  This site boasts the world's first virtual newsreader. There is fast, clear reporting, and the site is quick and easy to navigate.

In addition to these main sites there are many **alternative sites**. For example, following the September 11th terrorist attacks on New York in 2001, the following perspectives were available on the net:

- The United States perspective, with information about the war on terror, the bombing of Afghanistan and the search for Osama Bin Laden was available from:

  - CNN *(www.cnn.com)*
  - the CIA *(www.cia.gov/terrorism)*
  - the White House *(www.whitehouse.gov)*
  - the FBI *(www.fbi.gov)*.

- A website run by American Afghanis, *www.afghan-web.com* gave a very different picture of Afghanistan from the one portrayed in the Western media – that of a country full of bearded men carrying rifles.

- Small independent sites such as IndyMedia *(www.indymedia.org),* and Mediachannel *(www.mediachannel.org)* offered alternatives to the mainstream media and were completely independent of government influence.

- A Muslim newspaper produced in the UK, *www.muslim-news.co.uk/news,* ran an online section dedicated to reporting of the September 11th attacks from a Muslim perspective.

- An Arab site, *www.arab.net/links/welcome,* offered links to every Arab country in the world.

- The Muslim Student Association, *http://msanews.mynet.net/Scolars/Laden* presented Western and Islamic opinions on Bin Laden and his holy war.

Many Muslim sites provided considerably fuller background coverage of the Afghan conflict than the often patchy efforts of the western media. Two such sites were Islam Online *(www.islamonline.com)* and Islamicity *(www.islamicity.com)*.

It was also possible to find out about a range of Chinese opinion on the crisis at *www.china.org.cn/english/*.

Chatrooms

Technological innovations such as **chatrooms** can provide great opportunities for ordinary people to debate and express their opinions.

Sites such as *www.outtherenews.com* provide a diary for the public to enter debates – or simply to rant. This site was started in 1997 by a journalist, Paul Eedle, working from a converted attic in Muswell Hill, London. Eedle wanted to provide a forum where ordinary people could tell their own stories in their own terms 'without journalists getting in the way'.

READING THE MEDIA | Analysing computer games

There are many different kinds of computer game, each with its own distinctive conventions. Choose one genre and describe how it differs from all the others.

The following genre titles were taken from a computer gaming magazine:

- ▶ *action adventure*
- ▶ *science fiction*
- ▶ *flight simulation*
- ▶ *management*
- ▶ *first-person shooter*
- ▶ *space simulation*
- ▶ *racing*

- ▶ *role-playing*
- ▶ *real-time strategy*
- ▶ *puzzle*
- ▶ *sports*
- ▶ *action strategy*
- ▶ *chaos theory.*

These genres are not always clear-cut. A game can fit into more than one category. For example, a 'space simulation' could also be a type of 'science fiction' game. A 'first-person shooter' game could also be an 'action adventure'. The definition of a particular genre is a three-way process involving the game's producers, the professional critics who review the game for the media and the person who actually plays the game.

Choose a computer game you play which contains characters and analyse it using the guidelines below.

*Describe the **characters** and the functions they perform. For instance, are there any characters who perform the following functions:*

- ▶ *the helper*
  the trickster
  the magician
  the mother figure

- ▶ *the damsel in distress*
- ▶ *the father figure*
- ▶ *the dragon hunter?*

If there are heroes and villains, describe them in terms of ethnic origin, nationality, gender, physical appearance and virtues/faults.

If there are **villains**, do they tend to belong to particular ethnic or national stereotypes? Are you encouraged to be the villain? For example, in Hitman 2 the player is urged:

> 'Enter the mind of a genetically-engineered assassin-for-hire, whose deadly efficiency is now needed more than ever. Lured back into a global ring of deception by a twisted Russian crime boss, he must kill not only to make a living, but to continue living. This time it's not just business. It's personal.'

How are **heroes** or **superheroes** portrayed? Is the hero dedicated to protecting society against evil?

How are **women** represented, if at all? Are they active or passive, victims or leaders? If there are heroines, what sort of heroines are they? How are they dressed? What poses do they adopt?

How far is the game targeted at a male or female market?

Describe the **environments**, e.g. urban streets, forests, caves, and explain their purpose.

Are there any common **oppositions**? For example:

▸ good/evil	▸ primitive/advanced
▸ nature/science	▸ night/day
▸ east/west	▸ forest/desert
▸ brain/brawn	▸ plains/mountains

What sorts of **storylines** are there? Do they tend to start off with a problem or challenge and then introduce complications? Do the stories have endings? Do some games have basic linear storylines? Does this make them less interesting to play than those which have complicated sub-plots?

Discuss whether the playing of computer games has any **effects** on the players themselves.

> A report by the Independent Television Commission in 2000 entitled Copycat Kids? found that the media and especially TV, along with sport, pop music, computer games and 'hanging out with friends', formed the main components of youth culture. It concluded that imitation of behaviour depicted in the media does happen, but left open the question of whether this imitation is good or bad.

Describe an example of a game which is a spin-off from films or television.

Increasingly, the film industry relies on blockbusters to provide the bulk of its profits. These films generate a host of other merchandise such as T-shirts, caps, bags, mugs and sometimes computer games. For example, Spiderman: The Movie was a game issued to coincide with the release of the film of the same name in the UK. The plot of the game adheres closely to that of the film.

MAKING THE MEDIA · Design the main character for a computer game

Describe the role the character will play. For example, he/she might protect something, search for something, seek revenge or solve mysteries.

Draw the character and describe what powers and qualities he/she has.

Define your target audience.

▶ *Who will be interested in this new character?*
▶ *Which publications are most likely to be read by your target audience?*

*Design a **print advert** with your character in a new game.*
*Mention in your advert some of the **attractions of the game** to make the reader want to play it. For instance, look at the advertisement opposite for the spoof game Return to Castle Wittgenstein.*

*Describe some **scenarios** from your new game which involve your character. Produce simple illustrations to show **settings** and situations.*

Opposite: advert for the spoof computer game, *Return to Castle Wittgenstein*

FROM THE MAKERS OF **BERTRAND RUSSELL'S MONKEY TENNIS** AND **EXISTENTIAL ANGST TYCOON** COMES A REASONABLY ENTERTAINING SHOOTER WITH ADEQUATE GRAPHICS...

RETURN TO CASTLE
Wittgenstein

Return to Castle Wittgenstein is the tale of a renegade philosopher on the edge – a maverick who doesn't play by the rules – a desperate man who must now return to a zombie-infested castle in deepest Austria to wreak revenge. His mission is to defeat the evil menace by explaining to them that they cannot exist, as all analysis on the concept of mind is based on an acute category mistake: the idea that simple reports of subjective individual experience are primary sources for human knowledge. All this brave thinker has at his disposal is an arsenal of impenetrable texts, an atomic sentence gun, a kebab, three logic grenades and a pocket Heidegger.

With these tools and a stern belief that Philosophy is a load of old gibber, he sets out to bring stern justice to the nonsense of Castle Wittgenstein.

FULL 3D METAPHYSICS!

ADEQUATE GAMEPLAY!

"Whereof one cannot speak, thereof one must be silent."
PC GAMER

"Brains..."
PC Bones

"What them said."
PCP

"The graphics are mental!"
Friedrich Nietzsche

REAL-TIME BELIEF SYSTEM!

Features include:-
- Flamethrower zombies!
- Philosophical Zombies!
- Tractatus Logico-Philosophicus!
- Leather-clad Nazi girls!
- Trained philosopher!
- Machine-guns!
- Beetles in boxes!
- Mind body problems!
- Free Language games!
- Trees falling down in a forest!
- The sound of one hand clapping!

It's **All Over...**
...UNTIL THURSDAY 14TH MARCH

Design a web page.

Note: In order to design a website you need to have software programmes such as *Microsoft Frontpage, Adobe GoLive,* or *Dreamweaver*. Although it is possible to learn the basics of HTML (HyperText Markup Language) from Webmonkey at *http://hotwired.lycos.com/webmonkey/*, it is preferable to use the software packages above, because they allow you to create your web pages without complex programming code.

Look at some of the following sites to find ideas and inspiration:

▸ About.com Teen Advice*: http://teenadvice.about.com/*
▸ Cyberteens*: http://www.cyberteens.com/*
▸ So*: http://www.bbc.co.uk/so/*
▸ Google Teen Life*: http://directory.google.com/Top/Kids-and-Teens/Teen-Life/*
▸ A Girl's World*: http://www.agirlsworld.com*
▸ About.com Music for Teens*: http://teenmusic.about.com/*

Content

*First of all, make sure you have **something to say**. Your web pages must be worthwhile reading for somebody somewhere. What do you know about, or have experience of, which other people would be interested in? This could be:*

▸ *information*
▸ *fun or amusement*
▸ *advice or help*
▸ *opinions and views.*

*Try to keep to **one main theme** and make it clear to your audience what your site is focusing on.*

Presentation

▸ *Don't clutter your pages with too much information or decoration. Use **white space** (space without text or graphics) to make things stand out.*
▸ *You can only display one web page at a time, so you must **signpost** (label) each page clearly so that readers can tell quickly what interests them.*
▸ *Look at magazine covers and newspaper front pages. Note how they attract readers and make it easy for them to decide if they want to read on.*
▸ *Your home page should have a clear **title** and a list of **contents** or headings that readers can move on to.*
▸ *Look at the Tripod site (http://www.tripod.lycos.com). The home page is an excellent example of signposting and the site gives access to tuition, advice, ideas and a free image gallery with clip art, backgrounds, photos, lines, arrows and bullets, all of which can be pasted into your own site.*
▸ ***Pictures** will make your page more interesting, but remember that large pictures will take time to download.*
 *Keep **loading time short**. Potential website visitors will not like waiting even 10 seconds. Try to keep your entire page to around 30k. Images should be between 6-8 k. Each additional 2k adds a second to the loading time.*

Navigation

*Help people to **navigate** through your pages.*

▶ *To do this you need to build in internal **links**, which enable readers to choose which page they want to read without having to look through everything you have written.*

▶ *Consider **readability**. The eye travels from top left to bottom right. Any graphics you place on the page should assist this natural reading pattern, not hinder it.*

▶ ***Faces** should 'look' towards the centre of the page, not outwards.*

▶ ***Navigation** bars are better on the left of the page.*

▶ *Avoid having too many words in a single line. It is better to use **columns** as newspapers and magazines do.*

▶ *Don't use lots of different **fonts**, as this disturbs the reader. Plain fonts such as Arial, Times, Garamond and Courier are better than fancy ones.*

▶ *Make a **template**. This is a basic plan for each page, with space for text, graphics, your site's logo and name and links to the main menu. Having a pattern through your pages will make your site look tidier and will make downloading quicker.*

*Write an **evaluation** of your pages.*

State how you chose your target audience and how you tried to interest them. How effective was your production and what changes would you make?

For advice on writing evaluations, see page 51.

Exam practice ▬▬▬▬▬▬▬▬▬▬

Computer games

Look carefully several times at the opening sequences of the computer games *Spiderman: The Movie* and *Batman: Vengeance*. Then answer these questions.

1. What genre (type) of games are these? How can you tell?
2. How do the openings attract the player's attention? What pleasures, experiences and challenges do they promise?
3. Compare and contrast the main characters.
4. Describe in detail a challenge which either of the characters could face, using illustrations if you wish.

Index